MY PRESENT...
MY BATTLE WITH HEART DISEASE

by

David L. Reed

authorHOUSE™

1663 LIBERTY DRIVE, SUITE 200
BLOOMINGTON, INDIANA 47403
(800) 839-8640
WWW.AUTHORHOUSE.COM

First published by AuthorHouse 09/14/04

ISBN: 1-4184-9538-7 (sc)

Printed in the United States of America
Bloomington, Indiana

This book is printed on acid-free paper.

This book is dedicated to all the doctors, nurses, rehab specialists, EMT's, and all the other medical professionals who specialize in the care of patients with heart disease. I also dedicate this book to all those who have not yet been diagnosed with some form of HEART DISEASE.

I would like to thank the folks at All Saints Cardiovascular Institute, in Racine, Wisconsin for supplying me with their "Healthy Check-up" newsletter articles located between each journal. These articles are based on facts that all of us need to understand and live by.

For Janey, my love and my friend...
Thank you for being you.

This book shares the thoughts of a man who smoked cigarettes, sometimes two packs a day. He worked hard but never exercised. He drank too much alcohol, coffee and soda pop. He loved to eat, and really enjoyed it. His diet consisted of all the so-called good foods including:

- Steak, of large sizes and varieties
- Hamburgers, loaded with everything
- Bratwursts and sour kraut
- Ribs, any way they came
- Hotdogs and buns
- Ham, and lots of it
- Eggs, four to five any style
- Fast food restaurants and that entire menu
- Buffets, all you can eat
- Fish fries, with good tasting batter
- Snacks and dips
- Pies, cakes, sweet rolls and all the sweet goodies
- All this washed down with lots of milk, coffee, pop, wine, beer or whiskey.

At the age of 43, heart disease struck. He survived quadruple bypass surgery and now lives a heart healthy lifestyle.

He shares the secrets of his success (and much, much more.)

THE COVER PICTURE IS OF THE HEART PILLOW THAT WAS GIVEN TO ME AFTER SURGERY. I USED IT TO HOLD MY CHEST WHENEVER I COUGHED OR SNEEZED... VERY PAINFUL! SOME OF MY FAMILY AND FRIENDS SIGNED IT MUCH LIKE YOU WOULD A CAST. THIS PILLOW REMINDS ME OF THE ORDEAL OF QUADRUPLE BYPASS SURGERY. THIS REMINDER GIVES ME THE COURAGE AND MOTIVATION TO CONTINUE THE NEW LIFE I'VE CHOSEN TO LIVE.

About the Book

In this, his first work, Dave Reed brilliantly captures the essence of the profound physical and spiritual renewal waiting deep inside us all. Suddenly challenged by the major life crisis of acute heart disease with all its grave ramifications, Reed could have simply given in to fear, or anger, or worse yet, resignation. Instead, we read of Reed's courageous determination to change his life, which inspires the reader to turn each and every page. Ultimately, all who read this uniquely honest and personal self-examination will find themselves sharing in the joys of Reed's transformations. This is a story of almost impossible change, of the zest for life and for living well, and of the powerful new attitudes, which conquer old habits. Most importantly, Reed's story reminds each of us of the true hero that lies within, temporarily clouded by life's choices, just waiting for the motivation and desire to be unleashed. A truly remarkable read!

-Dr. Tim Dosemagen, Author, 'Prodigies - A Warring Species And The Human Heart', and 'The Impossible - A Collection Of Short Stories And Essays'.

Table of Contents

Introduction

Who knows what the **future** holds? No one! Do you know what your own **past** held? I do, now! So I think I'll call this **"My Present..."**

Hello, my name is Dave Reed. These so-called bunches of words compiled on paper have been assembled to try to share the story about this past year of my life. This story is based on 100% fact on what it was like to discover that I have heart disease and how I decided to deal with it.

The chapters are really journals I kept as thoughts of people and certain issues raced through my mind. Many of these issues may upset some of you. These issues are exactly what went through my mind as I battled with withdrawal of nicotine, alcohol, caffeine, red meat and sweets of all kinds. The biggest battle however, was facing the truth head on.

One year ago I weighed 292 pounds and was pleased with myself. I had dropped 20 pounds since that past Thanksgiving Day (312 lbs). I was very heavy. My blood pressure a year ago was 165/120 and my total cholesterol more than a year ago was 254, and my LDL at 180. I now weigh in at 205 to 210 pounds, my blood pressure is 116/78 and my total cholesterol is 129, and my LDL is 88. This is a major improvement. A year ago I wore size 46 pants and 2XL shirts. Now I wear size 36 pants and large to extra large shirts. I no longer crave nicotine, alcohol and caffeine. Red meat and sweets are now used as a treat and very seldom.

I hope you can find a use for some of this, as it means a lot to me. One whole year wrapped up in a couple hours' worth of reading.

This is just the beginning of a new commitment. I intend to live a heart healthy lifestyle. I want to tell the world how heart disease has changed my life, for the better, and to live the rest of my life for the "One" who gave me life again.

One year, for many of you, may not seem like a justifiable time frame for someone to make a full life change and commitment. I have the ingredient needed for this type of turn around. I want to live!

Journal No.1- April 1, 2003

Hello to all my friends and family. Just a note to update you on my so-called new lifestyle. I haven't felt this good or positive in a long time! I know a lot of questions are still out there, so let me try to sum up exactly what happened, now that I understand it myself.

For the past six months or so I hadn't been quite myself. I wasn't feeling right. Two weeks before Janey, my wife, and I had our annual vacation at the Wisconsin Dells, I started having chest pains. They would come and go every couple of hours and gradually got closer, lasted longer and were a bit more painful. I couldn't hide it anymore and finally told Janey what was going on. She insisted we go to the hospital right then and proceeded to throw me over her shoulder, load me up in the car and drive my complaining, 290lb so called body to the hospital here in Burlington. Well, needless to say, I continued to complain while the ER nurse was checking my vitals, when she told me that I wasn't too young to be having some kind of heart problem. That kind of hit me square between the eyes (legs, whatever), and all those questions about family history, past chest pain experiences, smoker, alcohol, cholesterol, diet, and all that stuff really made me stop and think! They took blood tests and an EKG and then X-rays and then the waiting game... ... ... The doctor finally came in and explained he was not sure what was going on and wanted me to spend the night. I asked if he thought it was my heart, and he didn't know. Then he told me I'd have to go to Elkhorn Hospital because they were filled up!

That did it --- I blew my cork and told them to unhook me and I was out of there!!! I did follow up the next morning with a stress test with the cardiologist. He told me it was a great and strong test and my heart was fine. He set me up with some pills for gas and sent me on my way.

It's funny how one's body acts so much like an old car... whenever you hear those annoying sounds under the hood and then you make an appointment with the mechanic, the clunking goes away!

So to the Dells we go. Sunday and Monday go by with the usual pain in the chest. The gas pills and Tums don't seem to be working and the corned beef dinner just didn't seem appealing. The pains were hitting hard every 10 to 15 minutes, so Janey called Dr. Sharon Smith back at home and then hauled my fat body into ER at St. Claire's in Baraboo. They proceeded to do the same exact testing I just went through in Burlington but insisted I go to Madison to St. Mary's because they did feel there was something wrong with my heart and additional testing was needed. The Doc called the other Doc and they agreed that it was time to have a heart catheterization performed. They both treated it as an emergency and had me transferred by ambulance to Madison (no lights or siren). That was a cool trip!!! I was feeling good and had no pain. The EMT's and I had a ball! I think that team of people are some of the finest bunch of medical staff I've ever seen. They also showed my heart scans to me and explained how the different lines reacted, showing distress or normal reactions. They were great all the way through! The driver even made sure she could see Janey following behind even when they're not supposed to.

Once delivered and all the same old questions gone through yet again, as well as registration, Dr. Kenneth Wallmeyer came in and finally explained to me and Janey just what the heck was going on inside this rather large gas-filled frame of mine. We agreed to the heart catheterization for first thing in the morning. He was confident that, yes, I had some sort of blockage and that he would be able to do an angioplasty if needed right then and there. I agreed, signed all the paperwork and prepared for the next day.

Well, we went through the procedure and the good doctor said, oh, boy, look what I found. He looked at me and said, there's more there than we thought! He then consulted another doc and they both agreed bypass surgery was needed. It turns out I had a 98%, a 95%, a 60% and a 20% blockage in my left coronary artery. No wonder I was not feeling so good!

The stress test in Burlington never picked it up! We have been told that is common.

Once again, the medical staff was totally awesome. They are a true team of experts and treated me like a human being, not just another broken heart. They explained every detail before it happened and made me as comfortable as possible. After cleaning me up from the heart catheterization, Dr. Wallmeyer came and explained what exactly had happened to me and I was now classified as high risk with severe heart disease. **I did not have a heart attack**!

He also explained that a cardiac surgeon had been notified, Dr. John Snider, and assured me that he was one of the best. I had no reason to question.

As you can imagine, this is when life got pretty interesting. Janey was strong, or at least tried to show that. I knew better and finally agreed with her to contact family. Before long, a lot of visitors were dropping in and the phone ringing off the hook. Man, I could've used a smoke and a beer or two!

Finally I met Dr. Snider and instantly trusted him. He reminded me of me! Same attitude and age yet a pro. Confident with his ability and my determination to get better, I felt very secure! So he explained in detail everything involved with bypass surgery and answered all the questions both Janey and I had. The only thing left to do was to get it scheduled. After a long couple of hours, the nurse came in and said, "you're set!" You must have a bigger hurt than anyone else on the floor 'cause you're going first in the morning. I said "cool, lets get it done!!!"

The rest of that evening was busy. Between the phone calls and visitors and nurses prepping me with info and meds, I never had a chance to think about me, just about all of you, and that was as rewarding as anything I've experienced in my entire life!

Finally I had a moment alone and upon reflection realized, holy... this is big! What if I don't make it? I'll be honest, that thought lasted for a very brief moment as I had a short talk with God and I knew all would be fine even if I didn't make it. I thought about my life and was fairly happy with myself, all except for one very important person, my daughter. I didn't feel that I had been a good dad to her all her life. I tried at times but never enough. I thank God that she was there with me that night, her and Brian (her husband), so I could share that with her. We hugged and teared up and now I think we've been closer than either of us knew.

I slept great, I felt good. I was looking forward to an even better life.

Five a.m. came pretty quick. I woke up to the largest black man I've ever seen standing next to me taking blood. He was smooth. I never felt the needle!

Then one nurse came in after another with more meds, shaving my chest, arms and legs, getting a final suppository, and finally a well-needed shower.

Janey and Stevie, my stepson, got there early and as always were by my side. Jennifer and Brian also came in and I felt special. The anesthesiologist had already done his job and the effects were starting to take. 7:15 and I was on my way. Kisses and hugs to all, and, of course, some kind of remark trying to ease out and stay relaxed for my family.

I remember looking around the operating room and being amazed at all the equipment. Another nurse came by and asked me if I was still awake, gave a shot of whatever and I don't remember anything until I heard someone say, "he's coming to now", and shock hit me or something 'cause I'm told I panicked and fought, and that breathing tube and I just did not see eye to eye. I remember all who came into ICU to visit. I remember the touching and comments, such as when my dear mother-in-law rubbed my arm and assured everyone that would comfort me, and I thought to myself, Dave, squeeze her back, so I did, and I think she was shocked 'cause she jumped and told everyone, "he knows we're here, he just squeezed me!"

I remember my nurse, Aaron, telling me to shape up, I'm scaring my wife. I was glad they strapped my hands down. I told them to do that before I went down. I knew I'd rip everything out if not strapped down. I guess I wasn't handling the pain very well. At this point everything is still foggy and Janey tells me things I kind of laugh at now.

Finally they pulled that nasty tube out of my throat and it was like I finally started to really come out of it. They told me to say something loud and clear to get my vocal cords working and Aaron told me that Janey was just outside the door, so, of course, the first words out of my mouth were "hey, Babe, get your butt in here and give me a kiss"! (I guess you had to be there). I didn't realize at that point in time that more than 24 hours had gone by. I lost a few hours somewhere.

Aaron started me on ice chips and believe me, nothing could've tasted sweeter. Then finally water and then even a small liquid lunch. Sara, who assisted throughout, said I really gave them a run for their money. Rough night. I felt bad for Janey. Then I was really getting myself back and asked if I could get out of bed and stretch out. Boy you would think I had just run a touchdown with the reaction I got from the entire ICU staff! Aaron asked me if I was sure 'cause usually they fight to get patients up for the first time. "Let's do it" I said, and away we went. I even took a few steps around the room, and Aaron, in full excitement for me, told me enough for now. It felt good, yet still weak. I wanted more so I could feel stronger, but I had to be patient.

Shortly, they got the okay to move me out of ICU and into my own room. It was really cool how Aaron introduced me to my new nurse. He pushed my chair into my room looked at Sue and said, "watch this." He looked at me and said, "get in the bed yourself." So I got up and on the floor, with his help, and crawled onto my new bed! (Apparently my version is not the same as Janey's. Hers sounds better and I'm sure is more accurate, since I was still pretty doped up at the time, but that's how I remember things.)

The staff at this place is exceptional. I can't stress that often enough. Talk about the best customer service I've ever seen...Aaron and Sara, thanks again for everything!

Within the next couple of hours Sue and Sara wanted me standing up again, and I did, and, of course, asked if we could go for a walk. They were a little worried 'cause once again that's not the way it's done, but we went for a walk around the room and out to the hallway before they bedded me down. An hour later we actually walked down the hallway for a bit and once I got down wind of all the positive comments, there would be nothing stopping me now! It felt good and my wife was smiling and my kids were proud. That was a long sore first day out of ICU, and the support I had from family just kept making me stronger and stronger. You guys are awesome!

When Dr. Snider came in, he was very happy with my progress and of course, reminded me of what I had been through. He asked me if I felt like "I was hit by a truck." I agreed and he reached out his hand to mine, shook it and said, "sorry, I was the driver" and assured me that I'd feel much better before too long. What a guy.

The next couple of days went by fairly quick with lots of walking, the entire wing all on my own, with the staff cheering me on like I was in training for a major event (called life.) There were lots of tests and cleaning of the wounds and training for going home and taking care of myself.

The drugs were finally wearing off and my brain actually started working again. I took a moment on one of my many hikes and thanked God for being there, not just for me but also for all of you too. All the visits, the phone calls, all the cards, are wonderful. One doesn't often take the time to say thank you. Well, I am right now THANK YOU ALL FOR YOUR HELP, CONCERN, PRAYERS, and SUPPORT and LOVE!!! I'm trying real hard not to mention anyone's name because I don't want to forget or leave anyone out. You know who you are and I know also. I've got the rest of my life to talk about it with you when we can share private time together.

Finally, the big day! Dr. Snider comes in and asks, "are you ready to get out of here"? "You bet," said I. He complimented my speedy recovery and still warned me to be careful, and, no driving until our next appointment in two weeks. I thanked him and away we go. Of course it took forever to get checked out (shift change). Got to admit, it was a little scary leaving the security of the finest bunch of people I have ever met! My deepest thanks and appreciation go to Dr. Smith, Dr. Wallmeyer, and to Dr. Snider. You saved my life! I will not waste your time.

This coming Tuesday I start my rehab at St. Mary's, All Saints Health Care Medical Center in Racine.

Some of you may know this and some may not but before the Dells I had sent my resume to Lambeau Field's Atrium. They sent me a nice letter back (putting me in the file), but at least I gave it a shot, and that is extremely rewarding all by itself, not to mention how good I felt after reading two of three reference letters. Thank you guys again! I can't wait to get back to work... I love my job!

 My Grandma died last night and we all thank God it's over! It will be my pleasure to write and read some words for her service this weekend in Kaukauna, WI. I'm sure her and Grandpa are happy together again.

Carol, who was married to our deceased son, Michael, and Justin, her fiancé, will be moving to Maryland this summer. Justin joined the military, and that will be his base. We are really going to miss Angel and Reina, our granddaughters. I sense larger phone bills and new vacation destinations in the future.

That's it for now. This journal writing idea came from one of the chaplains in Madison. He said writing things down would keep things in perspective and give me something to do when I'm bored or I want a smoke and a beer. I will try to keep all of you posted if and when things change or whatever.

Thank you all again for everything!!!

HOME - WHAT A PLACE!

Dave

The next two pages are the letters from Dr. Snider and Dr. Wallmeyer to Dr. Smith my family doctor. These letters explain in detail exactly what happened to me. The picture following Journal #2 is a heart diagram roughly giving an idea of where the blockages were and where the bypasses were made. The "bed" picture is what we heart patients wake up to after surgery. It is just as uncomfortable as it looks. In between the individual journals are the articles provided by All Saints HealthCare of Racine, Wisconsin.

April 2, 2003

Sharon Smith, M.D.
432 James Street
Burlington, WI 53105

RE: DAVID REED
DOB: 09/08/1959

Dear Dr. Smith:

I had the pleasure today of visiting with Mr. David Reed and his wife. As you recall, while vacationing in Wisconsin Dells, the patient was diagnosed with severe three-vessel disease and angina and subsequently underwent urgent coronary artery bypass grafting on march 20, 2003, at St. Marys Hospital in Madison. He did well and was discharged a few days later. Today he returned for a regularly scheduled follow-up appointment.

Overall, Mr. Reed has made an outstanding recovery, which is consistent with his young age and state of good health. He has taken no narcotic analgesics since he went home and his appetite has returned to normal and his bowel habits are regular and he has no difficulty with shortness of breath or other anginal type symptoms.

On examination today, his blood pressure is 110/66 and pulse is 76 and regular. The median sternotomy is healing well per primam and is stable. His heart has a regular rate without murmur, rub or gallop. His lungs are clear to auscultation bilaterally. His radial artery harvest site in the right upper extremity is healing well per primam.

He has made an excellent recovery following his surgical revascularization. His medications remain metoprolol 100 mg p.o. b.i.d.; Zocor 20 mg p.o. q.h.s.; Percocet which he no longer takes; Colace and aspirin one daily.

I am very pleased with Mr. Reed's recovery, as is he. I told him it would be okay to start driving at this point and to refrain from lifting objects greater than 10 pounds until June 1. He is to see Dr. Wallmeyer in the next two weeks and then will pursue cardiac rehabilitation and further cardiovascular care administered through your office. He will begin cardiac rehabilitation in St. Marys Hospital in Racine.

Thank you for allowing me the privilege of participating in the care of this delightful gentleman. I have enjoyed getting to know him and his wife. If you have any questions regarding Mr. Reed or any of your other patients, please do not hesitate to contact me.

Sincerely,

John M. Snider, M.D.
Department of Surgery
JMS/kl 3773687
C: Kenneth Wallmeyer, M.D. – Cardiology, Dean Clinic

SHARON SMITH, M.D.
432 JAMES STREET
BURLINGTON, WI 53105
April 3, 2003

Sharon Smith, MD
425 Milwaukee Avenue
Burlington, WI 53105

RE: DAVID REED
DOB: 09/08/1959

Dear Dr. Smith:

Mr. Reed is a 43 year old gentleman who is a supervisor at the YMCA in Burlington. I understand that you were consulted when he developed episodes of chest discomfort, and arranged a stress test in Burlington which was felt to be normal. Within days, however, while vacationing in the Wisconsin Dells area, he remained concerned with repeated episodes of chest discomfort, presented to the emergency department at St. Clare Hospital in Baraboo, and after consultation with us was transferred to St. Marys Hospital with a view toward definitive evaluation. While he remained free of any abnormal markers or obvious ischemic changes on his cardiogram, his symptoms did sound concerning and I pursued angiographic evaluation, frankly expecting not to find significant coronary disease. In the event, however, we found very severe obstruction of both his left anterior descending and left circumflex. The LAD lesion in particular was felt not to be amenable to angioplasty because of its being a "bifurcation lesion," with important involvement of the origin of the first diagonal as well. There would be the clear potential to lose an important diagonal branch if angioplasty was carried out.

Mr. Reed and his family expressed no hesitation in accepting advice for coronary artery bypass grafting, which was carried out. His postoperative course was brisk and uncomplicated.

Through all of this, we discussed at some length that stress tests are not perfectly sensitive, and that every cardiologist has been "fooled" by test results that fail to indicate the presence of significant disease. It would be my suggestion that Mr. Reed be referred for a nuclear stress test in two to three months after his surgery, both to document adequacy of revascularization as well as establish a baseline for future studies. The nuclear imaging would be particularly appropriate in view of some circumflex disease, which is often electrocardiographically silent, and his history of false negative EKG response. He will clearly benefit from statin therapy and aspirin indefinitely, but I anticipate return to full activities with no residual limitation.

If you have any further questions regarding his care here, or if I can be of any further help in follow-up, please don't hesitate to let me know.

Yours truly,

Kenneth W. Wallmeyer, M.D., F.A.C.C.
Department of Cardiology

KWW/cmc 3779466

Enclosure

CC:
SHARON SMITH, MD
425 MILWAUKEE AVENUE
BURLINGTON, WI 53105

Journal No. 2 - April 29, 2003

I would like to share a few thoughts I had while lying in the sun. This is a first for me. I've always worked in the outdoors, but I have never intentionally laid out sun-tanning. It feels great!

I'm not the same man I was six weeks ago. There have been so many changes and all at once. My moods have been challenged to the max lately. The medical folks tell me this is normal for heart patients. They tell me it takes three to six months before things settle down and that some things may never be as they were. My emotions have taken a toll. I feel so much more serious about all sorts of things, not just life itself. For instance, vices: Smoking, for example. I now understand how this affects our bodies. Rehab teaches us very well. I feel like a fool for letting myself go for so long. I know I'm human but, hey, we all know better, I did. Why do people fight themselves over addictions? I know how chemicals work on the brain, but I have to believe anybody who uses anything harmful has got to ask them self WHY or HOW can I stop? Those who say they enjoy these things are only lying to themselves and all their loved ones, especially the children, no matter what their age.

It seems to me one of three things will happen eventually. 1) You either get the help and support you need and change; 2) suffer some kind of medical trauma like a heart attack or stroke or a car wreck, and then you do something about it, (my case); or 3) you don't change at all and die, possibly taking someone else with you, or, at the very least, hurting your family and friends because you're gone for a foolish reason. (Seems to remind me of what suicide of someone you love feels like. It's a terrible waste and makes me very angry!) Nicotine, alcohol, pot, painkillers and all illegal drugs are addictive, and can we really keep the use of these things only at a "social" level? I don't think so. We may think we do, but who ya kidding? It's still killing parts of you each time you use. Enough of this, it makes me sick!

I look at people differently now. I wish there was something I could do, especially for those I care for. My opinion doesn't mean much unless you want it to.

Back to my emotions. Lately, sad stuff makes me cry and a good fart will bust open the hardest laughter I've ever had. Feelings for those I love and care for are enhanced beyond words. You have no idea how those little battles or arguments cut and hurt. Now I understand the "broken heart" theory. It's funny how all those usual disagreements seem so silly even when they used to seem so important.

I have so much more respect for those that are living a healthy lifestyle. I believe you can go overboard with this also, but I mean those who try to eat only healthy foods, exercise regularly and stay active. These people are always the ones you can count on. They usually seem to be happier and more successful. Other than drug or dope dealers, the healthy folks tend to have more money also. I'm finding that out as well. Its funny how a lot of people complain about not having enough money or time or things yet they always have plenty of beer, booze, pot or who knows what else! Think about it. These same people almost always have some kind of injury or ailment or simply just overweight, yet let's have another beer or get high... DAH!*!*

Just what do people need to be happy? TV can be okay if you like to watch sex, violence, game shows, dumb humor or possibly the few good shows that are on, of course your favorite collection of movies and obviously "Packer Football".

Lawn work and gardening for some is fun. Sports, whether you play or watch, is fun for all the seasons. Church and its activities, if you like that sort of thing, and all the arts and fine entertainment can all be fun things to do. But is that happiness? What about Family? Your spouse and kids are the true measure of one's own happiness. Every family has issues, good and bad, strengths and weaknesses and I do's and I don'ts with all. This is where every individual has the most positive and negative times in his or her life. Family time is the largest time spent for everyone and ultimately grooms our every day life and style. Even if you have no family, that certainly reflects. As kids we grow up with a certain kind of lifestyle from our parents and then the teenage years take us to new limits and we slowly start developing our own image and our own way of life.

For me, I'm not sure what happened. I always wanted to please my folks and my family. I always looked forward to helping out or always the one to count on or just be there in any matter that was needed. I loved to hear people say thanks and to feel that I was needed. I always tried to do my best at everything I did... Now I feel different. Please bear with me here. I don't want to hurt anyone's feelings, but I feel very alone lately, not lonely but just kind of out there all on my own where only a few can understand. What scares me are the people who care for me the most are the ones who hurt me the most and don't even know it! I know my family went through a rough time when I went down and I realize the fears you had and truly appreciate your love and support through this whole life-changing event, but I've changed. I'm not the same as before the surgery. That guy is gone and ain't coming back!

In order to survive and live on, major changes have been made. I've given up smoking. Think of all those times out on the porch or wherever and all the conversations we had that were framed around the duration of a cigarette. Most of those conversations opened up during or because of that time. That time is gone now. Replaced with long walks or something healthy. Having that beer or whisky and Coke is another vice left at the operating table. I still miss those so called "social times" of the day when people can unwind. Now I see it as catching a buzz or just simply getting stupid together. Many mistakes have been made during those times. GONE!

All I can say to those I love or who at least care for me is this: Deep down I'm still the same guy. Try to understand me like you used to, without all the vices. And when I say "deep down," I mean exactly that. I take life a lot more serious now. It's hard to tolerate things that hurt people. My affections need so much more attention and this feels like the greatest change of all! Making others happy and hearing the thank you are still important, but this is kind of like in second place right now. I don't want to seem greedy but right now I need to concentrate on ME and I need your help and understanding to get through this time. I do not, however, expect or demand anything from anyone. **I will do** this "new life" thing on my own, if needed. This statement can be read both as a positive and a negative. Please see the positive only. I really don't care for ultimatums, yet I just received a good wake up call and I'm trying to adjust and explain all at the same time.

At this point, rehab is going well and the staff at, All Saints Healthcare, are very helpful and patient with me. I keep pushing for more and they keep me at a safe and allowable rate. They've invited me to join them in the annual Lighthouse run/walk this summer. I still can't imagine that! Too bad I have to decline. It is the same weekend as the Camp Open House. I work for a YMCA camp, as the Maintenance Director. The class time at rehab is extremely educational. Mondays, proper exercise techniques and medical Q & A; Wednesdays, food and proper diet, Fridays, stress, how to eliminate, not just cope. This class is most interesting at this time in my life.

How does one eliminate stress? Avoid personal complications, stay fit in body, mind and spirit! Sounds like the YMCA (my employer). Being honest with yourself is the No.1 ingredient. If you say you are happy, then be happy, not just satisfied with things. Satisfaction is all too often accepted in place of happiness. We tend to get only so far in life with personal goals and usually end up "satisfied" at a certain point and ultimately stop short of our true goal and real happiness. The No.2 ingredient is love. Do we really know what love is (Forrest Gump), and do we really know how to love in return? Love – the most misused word in the world and the most unused word in the world! I believe there are many definitions for this one little magnificent word of feeling and emotion. It can be a noun or a verb. It can be an adjective or adverb. One thing for sure, when used properly, it provides security, commitment and true happiness!

I can't wait for the doctor's full release on June 1st when all my limitations, such as running, lifting and being a brute (retrained), will be lifted and I can again be in full Dave style. I've got way too much time to think about all this stuff, I'm really not the philosophical fool that I appear to be right now.

I am really looking forward to, and already beginning to, enjoy this new lifestyle. I believe it took me 43 years to finally figure out who and what I really want to be as I'm finally starting to grow up! You really can fix a broken heart. Always do the positive and avoid the negative. We all know the difference between right and wrong. We may disagree on certain issues, but deep down we all really do know better.

For me, the right thing is to get healthy and stay that way. I want to feel good again. I want to look good again. I want the energy back to keep up with all those kids I love and care for. This will make me HAPPY. Don't laugh, but I would like to live to be 103 years old. I know it's not my decision to make, but I'm going to live the kind of lifestyle that will allow me to live to be one of the oldest surviving coronary by-pass patients ever.

I'll keep you posted.

Dave

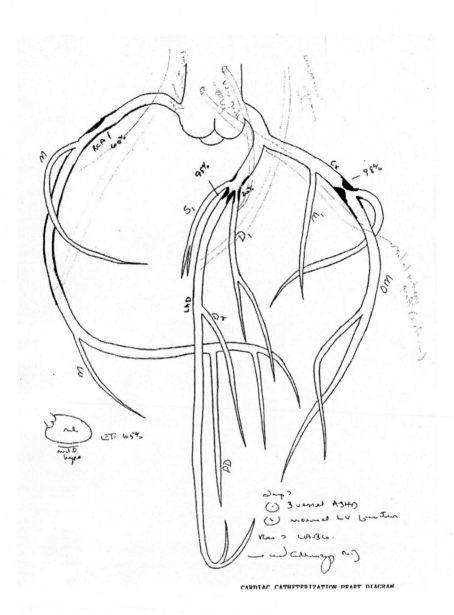

CARDIAC CATHETERIZATION HEART DIAGRAM

Journal No. 3 - 4th of July weekend, 2003

Three months and two weeks later, not to mention approximately another 15 pounds lighter, and still going strong. My doctors are very pleased and have thanked me for not wasting their time. They caution me and say time is on my side, but longevity is the true test. My next appointment is February or March 2004. I have a goal. I will be fit!

In Journal No. 2, I came down hard on vices and such. I didn't intend to be judgmental and if I was, it was directed at me, myself and I for falling into their slave type trap. I'm simply trying to communicate my thoughts and warn others of the sneaky death grip the vices have on us that indulge.

I'd like to share some more thoughts that are still going through my newly trained brain regarding my new lifestyle, but first I'd like to tell you how much I appreciate your responses and care and concern about my life. It means a lot to me. This helps motivate me to continue on and do what I know I have to do.

Rehab has been done now since May 21st and I still miss the careful, yet exhilarating, retraining process that those six weeks did for me. That's right, completed in six weeks! The Rehab staff, once again, is exceptional, and now that I'm on my own and continuing all they taught me, I can honestly say they are the greatest teachers in the world, at least in my world. I find that I correct myself when doing something differently than the way they showed me. The last session I had was truly a pacesetter and the greatest lesson learned. It was the hardest workout I've ever had in my life, as far as exercise goes. They gave me a choice; I could slack off, being my last day, or go the distance with my two favorite machines. All my so-called, classmates cheered for slacking off and leaving early and the staff said whatever I decide would be fine (sarcastically). I went for total completion and smoked the belts off those two machines! Ask my wife and my sister and they'll tell you...after all they are my best friends. (That's a different story I'll share soon.) Back to rehab. The lesson I learned, or should I say experienced is twofold. Choices are not as easy as they seem. I'll bet every one of you are thinking right now that I had no choice with that decision and the obvious choice to make was to continue working out the way I did.

Well, here is the way I see it. That decision was not made just for that day or moment in time, it was made for life. During the little graduation ceremony they gave afterwards, they told me I have no physical limitations except for one, snow shoveling, and I have no mental limitations unless I break down and listen to those who cheer for slacking off, even if they have good intentions. They reminded me that heart disease does not go away, you can only control it with medication, proper diet and exercise as trained. Who knows? I might just live to be 103. Then again I might not.

Back to the lesson. Ask yourself an honest question. Have I ever said "I won't do that," yet you did? Have you ever said "I'm going to do this and you didn't?" Of course you have, but that's just how easy it is to make the wrong choices in life. The beauty is this: Try not to make this a habit, and forgive yourself when you do and get back at it ASAP!

Never criticize or snicker at those who make a wrong or bad choice. Sometimes one just doesn't see the whole picture. Don't take for granted any choice one makes, including your self. Choices in life come in all different shapes and sizes, from a little lie to suicide, from a smile to a tear, from a dream to procrastination. I think I learned more about myself in those six weeks than the last 43 years.

One of these days I will stop and visit with the rehab folks at St. Mary's in Racine. Maybe I'll bring them a treat. Now, there's a choice, should I bring doughnuts or fresh fruit?

I've always heard how difficult it is to lose weight, and, boy, how true it is. I walk a minimum of three to four miles every evening and try to get in five to six miles when the time allows. That is the key to the whole program, when the time allows. I've restructured my lifestyle so I can get in at least one to one and a half hours every evening to walk and bike, and every other day do my dumbbells. Janey is trying to do the same. I do this at least six days in a row and take one day off to rest the muscles. I can step on the scale and watch pound after pound go off, but it takes about three to five days before you see one pound shed off. Then at night the scale reads three to four pounds heavier and the next morning is the true test. If you followed the diet 1800 to 2000 calories the day before and didn't cheat, the weight goes down. If you didn't follow or you were too close, some of that three to four pounds will stay with you until you burn it off again. The bad part about it is you can't work extra hard the next time to shed it off. It simply doesn't work that way.

My long-term goal is to drop 100 pounds by next March. That's 100 pounds in a year. Last Thanksgiving I weighed a whopping 312 pounds. I had started to lose weight over the winter, so I was 290 the day I went to Burlington Hospital. I really need to get down to between 200 and 210 and then re-evaluate. I now weigh 240 pounds. That's 50 pounds lost since surgery, and a heck of a good start. My short-term goal is to be 225 by September 20th, which will be six months and halfway there. The timing appears to be on my side, but in reality the first 20 pounds comes off easy compared to the last 20 pounds. You can lose the first 20 simply by changing your habits a little and watching the amount of food intake.

Then it gets tough. Now you're ready to make big changes, like calorie counting, workout routines and spending money on healthy foods (not to mention clothing). We all have tried to lose weight before and we get so far and ...the only word missing at this point, I've learned, is discipline. Man you got to want it bad! You need to have some kind of drive or incentive to keep going, and this brings me to my next thought.

I've actually been told that I'm lucky I have a reason to do what I'm doing! Others say, it's so hard to find the time, or it's easy for you Dave cause you've always been able to control your actions. Bull! I will not mention names but these statements have actually been said to me, and the best part, these comments came from family members!

Lucky. I hate this word and I think it should be outlawed. The only good use was a name for the cat on the T.V. show Alf. There is no such thing as luck, in my book. In the first place, whoever thinks I'm lucky might want to ask Janey if she thought I was lucky when she was told to leave the ICU room several times because things were getting tough and the nurses had their hands full with keeping me alive! In the second place, just because someone has accomplished goals he or she made doesn't mean they are lucky, it simply means that individual did what it took to accomplish the goal. Is that person unlucky if the goal was unattained? No. It does mean, however, that he or she did not work hard enough or is not quite done yet or maybe needs to re-evaluate the specific goal at hand. It has nothing to do with winning a lottery either. A whole lot of people buy tickets, correct? It only stands to reason that someone will be picked the winner or maybe no one will win that round. It's the same with car accidents. A good friend of mine, George, just got rear ended and rolled their SUV on the 894 bypass in Milwaukee and totaled it. No one got hurt, just bumps and bruises. His comment, simply put, the angels were watching over us. It has nothing to do with some kind of luck, good or bad.

We as individuals hold our own destiny in our own hands. Even when life- changing events hit us square between the eyes and break our hearts. I believe we still are in charge of whatever happens next, at least in our own minds and how we react. Let me give an example: Janey, my wife and my very best friend. Some of you know the tragedies that she has endured with her sons. Her youngest, Steve, lost a leg to bone cancer at the age of seven, and her oldest, Mike, took his own life at the age of 24 leaving a wall of pain and hurt that can never be brought down. Does this make her unlucky or does this make you lucky? I don't think so! We cannot control things that get dished out to us but we can control our own feelings and actions. And once we've accepted whatever it is that gets dished out, that is how we can control our own destiny again.

It is not easy. It hurts and is more painful than anything we can imagine. What am I talking about? Not any specific example. We all have had our own tragic moments in life. What I'm talking about is self-control. When we have a handle on things, even bad things, we're in control of our own path or destiny. Lord knows we get blown off track with tragic issues, but then we have the capability to move forward and challenge the next decision in front of us. The grieving process is a wonderful tool, and the only ingredient needed from others is time.

Janey is my inspiration. This woman has had more issues thrown at her than anybody I've ever encountered. She is still in grief and rightfully so. Time will prevail and I believe in her. She may not smile as much as she used to, but when she does, it's something special. She is a real lady and a compliment to the female society, not to mention the human race! Someday I hope I can find a way to tell her just how much I need her, but for now I will show her. When I saw the look in her eyes when the doctors gave us the "poop," I was afraid to be the next tragic moment in her life. This woman has had enough crap dished out to her to last three lifetimes. I pray that I can continue with my new lifestyle, not just for my sake, but also for hers. I need to out live her and I hate that thought, yet that's in God's Hands. Two people who need each other as bad as we do don't count on luck.

To bring it all together, luck has no meaning. The choices we make will promote and dictate what and who we are. If I'm right, then I'm on the road to a long healthy life, and if I'm wrong, then that makes me the Luckiest Man Alive!

I love being in a win/win situation and I love to share that excitement or rush with all of you, and especially my bride.

Recently I spent the better part of a weekend with my sister. Along with my wife, Mary is a true fan and believer in what I'm trying to accomplish. Her words of encouragement and pride also inspire me. I'm proud of these two women, as they have been there when I'm down and need a kick in the butt, or a hug to get me going again! I cannot fail with these two on my team. (They won't let me!)

So many of you have been so kind and understanding but these two have been "Extra Good" as Norm, my late step-dad, used to say.

Some of you may think I'm going overboard. But, I can't stress enough, the importance of living a heart healthy lifestyle and the effect of heart disease. If I had the power to keep that from happening, I would. But I don't. I can only try helping by telling you through these words and experiences. I'm just a man who doesn't want to see anyone else get cut open and run though the mill when you don't have to. But, hey, that's your choice.

Thanks for your time and support.

Dave

Just Say No to Tobacco Use

There is no doubt that using tobacco in any form is harmful to your health.

Whether you smoke it or chew it, tobacco use causes illness and death. In the United States, tobacco causes nearly one in five deaths, and more than 440,000 Americans die from the effects of tobacco each year. Almost 90% of lung cancer is caused by smoking. Smoking cigarettes increases the risk of heart disease, which is America's number one cause of death. Second-hand tobacco smoke (environmental tobacco smoke) is also dangerous.

Also, about 3,000 non-smokers die from lung cancer each year.

Children whose parents smoke are more likely to suffer from pneumonia, bronchitis, ear infections, and asthma.

Tobacco use is the single most preventable cause of death in our society. The good news is that stopping the use of tobacco increases your chances of leading a healthier life

Nicotine, a component of tobacco, is addictive. Quitting smoking is not easy and some people try several times before succeeding. Many of those who have tried to quit have done so on their own by either stopping "cold turkey," participating in the Great American Smokeout, or using other methods. There's no one right way to quit.

Quitting for good may mean using several methods including joining a support group, taking a class or using Nicotine Replacement Therapy. You don't have to do this alone. Talk with your healthcare provider for advice and support.

Journal No. 4 - August 20, 2003 - Five months later

Hello all! I have good news to share. I just stepped off the scale at 224 lbs. Wow!!! I'm a little ahead of schedule. Think I'll have a steak tonight.

I've been pondering on a thought, which requires your feedback. I will not use names, as I believe this will affect all of us on a different level. While out for one of my evening strolls, I was thinking about a certain person(s), and the trouble they were having with each other, when it hit me. There are two questions that constantly appear when people argue, don't see eye to eye, and totally disagree with each other. You get the idea. 1) What makes one person better than the other? Answer: At some things they are. 2) Why do we judge people instead of understand and accept? Answer: We need to be in control and it's human nature. These answers are short and not very sweet.

I've got six ways to look at any question that ever comes up: as a son, as a brother, as a father (parent), as a husband, as a grandfather (Bumpa) and as a fellow human being.

As a son, it was a learning experience; as a brother, a sharing experience; as a father, it is a teaching experience; as a husband, it's a loving, learning and a sharing experience; as a Bumpa, it's been great and a second chance to do it all again and better; and as a fellow human being, it's an amazing experience on both sides of good and bad.

I've been a son to someone twice in my life and I certainly can see parts of my dad, my mom and, yes, even a little bit of Norm, my step-father, in myself. They make up just a little bit of me, yet have steered, or should I say, taught me into my way of being. My parents know how I feel about them. They taught me everything I needed to know, to the best of their abilities, and supplied me with the tools (advice) to continue on with my quest or search of my own self. This is the basic role of a parent. Once this is accomplished, and the child moves out on his/her own, let him/her live, and watch him/her with loving eyes, and be there when he/she needs you UNCONDITIONALLY. In return always show the love and respect that they deserve. I walk on thin ice with this remark because so many kids never had good parents, which explains a lot of disrespect we see in some today and in the past. We all were treated somewhat differently as we were growing up, yet it's truly mind boggling that every one of us has the basic knowledge of right and wrong and good and bad. I think this is exactly the beginning of our equality as human beings. GOD still is and always will be amazing to me!

As a parent myself I often wonder what kind of children my parents were and what kind of parents they had, just to see the progression of life's standards and morals, not to mention the traditions that have stayed the same but also the new ones that have emerged. It's fun to look back at how I was raised as a son and to see the many differences I've incorporated in my parenting role today.

I've always enjoyed being a brother, not necessarily the oldest, but I think the world of all my brothers and my sister. We all grew up watching the other, in a way only we six can relate, and no one else in the world shares that bond, not even our parents. Being the oldest has some positives along with some negatives, but I'm here to ask you, just what can we do about it? I didn't ask to be first, or last for that matter. I can only live the way I've chosen and try to be an example for all people, not just my family. The same is true for my brothers and my sister. We all accept each other's way of life, and I believe there are six different opinions, not just in ways of living, but with everything imaginable. I believe that's the way it should be. Each and every one of us loves our own kids unconditionally and wants our children to be happy and loving individuals so they can someday pass it on. We may not all have a lot in common, but in some aspects, yes, we do, and I can honestly speak for all us Reed kids when I say we will not get in our children's way (as they get older), even when we know they're heading for trouble, or simply don't agree with THEIR DECISION. As parents it is our responsibility to warn and educate and let them be. When they ask for help, then we know we have done a good job as a parent, because they could have gone to someone else for help. Then, by God, you better come through 'cause it's never too late to lose their trust and respect.

Children and their parents, or is it parents and their children. This is double trouble when you're a parent and also someone's kid, and it really gets interesting, or triple trouble, when you are a grandparent. I really enjoy hearing about or observing my nieces and nephews; talk about a cool bunch of kids--I'm sorry, young adults. Watching or hearing about their lives, you can just see a little bit of their mother and father in them and waiting to see what they develop into is truly exciting. I wish I could be with them more but when we do see each other, it's a good thing and never enough.

I'm a dad and a pa. To my daughter Jennifer, I'm Dad and to my two step-sons, Mike and Steve, I have always been Pa, out of respect for their dad. That's cool. They have always known how I feel about them. I hope I've done right by them and I want them to know if there's anything I still need to do, just ask and we'll talk about it. I've always seen myself as a part-time father. I never had enough involvement with Jennifer in her childhood years, and none of "my blood" in Mike and Steve. I don't think that way anymore. Mike has found his peace, through suicide. I don't agree with how he found it, but just how do you define **UNCONDITIONAL LOVE**? Steve comes over and still asks for our opinion on some things and bounces off his latest thoughts or ideas, and Jennifer and I are still getting closer and talk several times a week about all sorts of stuff. Planning for a baby seems to be in her future. I love my kids and they love me. What's even cooler is I like my kids and they like me, too!

I've been a husband twice. The first time gave me Jennifer and taught me "how to" for my second time. I Thank God for Janey and you all know how I feel about her. I'm proud to have her as my partner in all of this and I'm pretty sure she feels the same. Hold on I'll ask her. Yup, whew!

Being Bumpa is really cool! I mentioned the second chance scenario before and I meant it. The beauty of being a grandparent is two-fold. Not only do you get the chance to see the young ones grow, you also get the ultimate second chance with your own kids.

In our case, with Mike, things didn't work out so well, but, hey, those two girls, Angel and Reina, mean more to us now than ever. We certainly have great times together. Janey and I will be flying out to Baltimore for my birthday weekend this coming month to spend a few days with them. It seems Justin will be transferred to Germany and Janey and I will be lost without them for a while. We'll pray for them and for ourselves for a speedy absence.

As far as being a fellow human being, well, that covers a whole lot of territory. All other relatives, some very close, and some you don't see or hear from very often, friends, church members, employer and employees, neighbors and everyday folks at the store, sidewalk, gas station and people driving by, the list goes on, but the same two questions affect us all the same and all in a different way at the same time. What makes one person better than the other or are we all equal? Why do we judge and evaluate people instead of understanding and accepting them for who they are? Be honest about this subject. If you think I'm wrong, tell me, but I think all of us just naturally have these thoughts, all on a different level perhaps, but just the same, still there. Maybe it's just me thinking too hard while pounding the pavement, or is the answer simply a part of our upbringing? If so, what's the cure? I'd like to hear your opinion on this, so please give it some thought and let me know.

While waiting for your response I'll give you a little of my opinion. After all this is my journal not yours, ha, ha. I'll be brief and get one thought out for now. One's ego is a strange thing. When this is mixed with our parents' versions of prejudices and shortcomings and that mindset we develop over our own individual likes and dislikes, then, holy cow, we don't stand a chance! Lord why did you create such horrible people? Man, we're gonna die! We sure are, someday, and we don't know when. So the old saying "Life is too Short" comes into play. Don't I know it! What's does this have to do with the two questions, you ask? Everything. Think about it and talk to me. I'm curious to find out how you all feel about this. Call it research!

Thanks for your time,

Dave

St. Mary's -
All Saints Health
care

- Racine

Risk Factors for Coronary Artery Disease

Your coronary arteries are the blood vessels that feed the heart itself.

Your heart gets the first supply of oxygen-rich blood from the lungs. And with all the work your heart does, it deserves the best. But sometimes these arteries get clogged. If a coronary becomes too clogged, then that part of your heart doesn't get the oxygen and nutrients it needs and you can develop chest pains when you exercise. Left untreated, a blocked artery can lead to a heart attack and even death. Usually there's not one simple cause for coronary artery disease.

You are at risk for coronary artery disease:

■ if your family has a history of coronary disease

■ if you have untreated high blood pressure

■ if you're obese or don't exercise regularly

■ if you have a stressful life

■ if you smoke OR

■ if your cholesterol and triglyceride levels are elevated.

or

Journal No. 5 – September 20,2003 - Six months later- seems like forever

Hello all. It has been one heck of an experience, to say the least. I'm not sure which part of me has changed the most, my physical self or mental self. Regardless, both are entirely different, I hope for the better.

My brother-in-law, Dave, asked me the other day how many miles I've walked since this journey began. I did some honest calculating and was rather surprised. 107 days at an average of four miles a day is 428, plus six weeks of rehab at an average of two miles a day, times six days a week is another 72 miles equaling 500 miles! Well, that answers the physical part of the change. The mental part equals 15 minutes a mile worth of thought. That's 7,500 minutes or 125 hours or just more than three 40-hour weeks at the office. No wonder things look different! No wonder I look and feel different!

Another friend, Rita, asked me, what would I do when my routine or diet started to get boring? Good question. I thought about it a lot and found myself rereading all these journals. I discovered the answer was within my own thoughts and experiences already. I hope and pray that will always be the case. With so many of you out there to help me keep focused, I can't imagine failure at this point. Some may argue that "you're only human, Dave", but I don't believe that is a negative as much as a positive attribute.

I really and truly feel great! The exercise program I've chosen is very exhilarating and makes me want more. The time I've had to think about things has been wonderful. I have seen every sunset and every moonrise for the past six months now. It makes no difference where you live. These two sights always make me Thank God for the beauty of his creation

I have never felt the fear of death yet and that has been my ongoing inspiration from God. He has given me a second chance in life, not in life vs. death. He would have taken me then if it was my time. This time I get to live the way I've always prayed for. He has answered my prayer! About seven months ago, when life was at a standstill, I was laying in bed praying to God to help me quit smoking, drinking, eating like a pig, among other things, and to give me the strength to do what I knew I had to do. There are some things I can't explain with words. These moments were very private and serious. I asked this of Him every night for a long time. Pardon the pun, but only God knows how long. Since then, I have to admit, my admiration, love and respect for His creations have grown immensely.

We are a society that creates many ways of doing things. In turn, as individuals, we have become creatures of habit and that is very hard to change or even accept for some of us. Remember the last journal with the question of why some people think they're better than others? I received several replies. Thank you. And without names or quotes, all the responses had one thing in common; I know a lot of kind people. These kind people, however, know some not so kind people and talked about, both specific and in general, happenings in their lives with people who think, "their stuff don't stink." You also reminded me of those unfortunate souls born into this world less fortunate than us. This whole topic really intrigues me because it is so in tune to my past lifestyle.

33

There is one word that brings it all together in my mind, balance. For every up, there's a down. For every right, there's a left or is it wrong? You get the idea. Me, I'm trying to balance out my life. Not that it was all bad. Heck no! I just need to improve or repair where it is needed. I found myself asking God for help because I know that I can't do it alone. He has given me the tools I need to fix this problem. He also put me in a place where I have to look before I cross or I'll get hit hard. God is the only "Judge" and we need him to be. We can only judge ourselves and live to the best of our ability. Well, if this is so, I've got many abilities and it's time I put them to work and at the best I possibly can. I will not be less than what I know deep down I can be.

This reminds me of a lecture from my dad years ago. I miss him more than anything. Yeah, I know he fell short of his goals, but did he? My dad died at the age of 51 from pneumonia. God has the only answer to that. I know Dad would have coached me through a lot of the hard times, and in a way he still is. What does a person do when he loses a parent? Dad told me a long time ago "you better learn how to take care of yourself, boy. No one else will." Including him!

Who do you turn to with questions and major life changing events? I count on God and the abilities that He and my parents, teachers, leaders, clergy, coaches, true friends and family instilled upon me. One of my favorite movies is the "Lion King." For the past 15 to 25 years or so I've had the privilege to work with many young people at both the YMCA and in Scouting. Since the movie "Lion King" came out one of the ways I would get to know these young people was to have them share with the group their favorite part of that movie. Funny how most of them actually had their own favorite part! Then they would ask me what mine was, and of course I would oblige, but with a twist. At the end of the movie, what did the monkey say to Simba? He pointed up the mountain and signaled Simba to take his place as "King" and said, "It is time"! Teachable moment for this guy. Ask any one of those kids and some are now Board members for MacLean and Scout Leaders for other kids. I explain to them how this reflects the same time of life they are each going through right now. They're walking the fence of childhood and being an adult. Time to choose. " It is time"! All of a sudden there is a new respect looming over all of them and I feel connected with each one of them, as an equal. Anyhow, that's my favorite part in the movie (as far as kids are concerned). My real favorite part is when Simba and Mufasa, his dad, are together after the rescue from the hyenas, father and son together, and nothing can get in the way. Looking up at the heavens together and promising each other things that even death can't take away. Yup, I sure do miss him (My dad, not Mufasa)! I really do know how he felt now, and that is his gift to me. I'm proud to be one of his sons!

So many things have changed in my life. Emotions like pain, laughter, happiness and sadness, all of them so real and so very intense. Notice the balance? When I feel happy, it feels warm and fulfilling. When I'm sad, I need to hide in fear of showing it. Confrontations are no longer intimidating. If we can't talk civilized, then we won't talk at all. Heartaches crush me into tears and humor makes me wonder for more. Life is too short to spend it bickering or fighting. I can't understand why some people push others away with their own ignorance, especially when we don't know God's plan! What if? Heaven forbid, but how would you feel if someone you loved or cared for died before the two of you patched up?

Attitude is another word with more than one face. I try to keep a positive attitude on everything. This is not always possible because I tend to get down on myself harder than I should. But I do try to stay positive and that helps me sort out good from evil and allows me to "keep the peace," sort of, between others. More importantly, it helps me keep myself in check. When I sense a bunch of others disagreeing with me and copping an attitude towards me, I call a timeout and check my way of thinking. Often I find myself accepting another point of view or opinion. This, however, does not necessarily mean I've changed my mind, but it does help me to better understand the beauty of being different, or in another word, "individual."

Life is too short, not for material things or possessions, but for personal accomplishments. We really are not here on this earth for that long and none of us know just for how long that is, so why waste any time?

You could say my prayer has been answered. You could say it's my second chance in life. You could say that I'm lucky. You could say I have no choice, but to change my life. I would agree. I would also say it would be greedy of me to not share it with you because I have learned such a great deal about so many things, including myself.

Enjoyment of life is on the top of my hit parade. I have a new niece, Maya Marie, born just a couple of days ago. My brother, Mike, called during the last Packer game to share the news of becoming a Grandpa. He is so proud of his daughter, Angie, and I'm sure he can't wait to see them or hear more very soon. She lives near Vegas and the distance creates unavoidable problems. Distance is a bear for all relationships.

This past weekend, Janey and I were in Baltimore visiting our two granddaughters. We spent the weekend together in a nice hotel and had a ball! We always hate saying goodbye and we always look forward to the next visit.

I have been smoke free, alcohol free, caffeine free and high cholesterol free for six months now. The next person that asks me what's left, I think I'll give them my right. There's too much to describe. You need to feel it yourself. "Freedom" and "in control" is as close in words I can get to describe the feeling of living this way. It is a whole new world for me, but not really. This is how I was when I was a kid who looked up to guys like Ray Nitchke, Bart Starr and the Kennedy brothers. Now I have young ones looking up to me, not to mention my own kids. That's cool, and I want to be the right kind of guy to be looked up to. Once again, that's why six months is not a lot of time, yet it amazes me how much one can do with it once one has the opportunity. I thank God again and again for this second chance and I still need His help to keep me going and going and going.

Work has been very good to and for me. I work for a YMCA camp as the maintenance director. I have found my niche in this world. Lambeau will have to wait. My co-workers have been very patient and my staff has been super. They have covered well for me and done their jobs without me having to bark. I'm proud of them! My boss, on the same hand, has been terrific. He knows what I've done with this turn-around in life better than anyone (except Janey). He has shown me a kind of respect that I truly admire. He doesn't treat me any different when it comes to my needed discipline. In fact, I sense his appreciation for my skills now more than ever. He lets me decide when I have had enough with anything and doesn't pacify me or make me feel like a wimp! He's a great quarterback or coach, and I'll receive for him any day for any game. He wants to win, which means this Camp will be the best!

However, I'm tired. It has been a very long summer. I'm going to take a little vacation this next week. I'll go up to my sister's place and do a little bow hunting, camping, some golfing and a lot of North Woods walking, get caught up on some naps and wrestle around with her kids. Hopefully I'll make it across the state and see some of my brothers and my aunt and their families. I miss all of them. Please feel free to drop a line or a word or two. Fall is coming quick and I plan to spend a lot of time outdoors, walking and enjoying the beauty of the season. Venison is a welcomed food to my diet and I look forward to that harvest and all the good times that go with it.

Go Packers!

Dave

David L. Reed

The Threat Women Face From Heart Disease

For years, heart disease was thought to be primarily a man's disease; however, we now know that heart disease is the number one killer of both men and women.

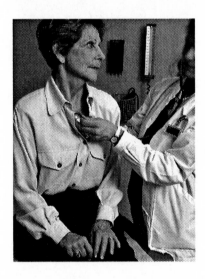

The symptoms for heart disease in men tend to be more obvious: a debilitating, crushing pain in the chest, an unannounced, sudden heart attack. The subtlety of women's symptoms – indigestion, fatigue, abdominal pain – makes it more difficult to diagnose although more accurate diagnostic testing has made a difference in the diagnosis of heart disease.

Treatment for heart disease in women generally follows the same line as for men: medicine, angioplasty and stents, and coronary artery bypass surgery are all effective and appropriate treatments for women with heart disease.

Journal No. 6 December 23, 2003 - nine months and a few days since surgery:

The new "Circle of Life" is about to be celebrated again on Christmas morning in a couple of days. I've a thought to share with all of you. No, more like a special feeling.

The past couple of years have been rather sad for Janey and I and yet somehow the spirit of life still burns stronger than ever, maybe because death has been so near to not just us but for all. Cancer in our child, the loss of my dad, then grandpa, then Norm, then Mike, and somewhere in there 911 and all the world in terror, a war, heart surgery then grandma. It just happens to make me think of another subject, the beauty of death!

How, you may ask, is death beautiful? The latest example and maybe the best example I can give was witnessed last night on Monday Night Football. That's right, Brett Farve's loss of his father and best friend. He and his family will most certainly suffer the pains of mourning. Sorrow is a humbling experience, yet also very rewarding. Look at how the entire nation surrounded that family in such a short time frame. While listening to the sports people report and talk about this matter, some of it should never have been said and some of it was very good. It all, however, was done out of respect, care and concern for that entire family. It is a beautiful thing! Brett's reaction was simply rewarding and justifying. He's a great football player and did what he does best. He played the best game of his life! But for who?

911 and all that turmoil! All the death surrounded by heroes of all different ages, creeds, races and the relationships that started, the pulling together as a nation even when people disagree; the discussions around dinner tables and or strategic planning tables; People pulling together for people they do not even know. Who are they doing this for?

These moments in life are what separate us from all other creatures. When bad things or disasters happen, the people around us do things to help. Some do a little and some do a lot, but all do what they can. That's beautiful!

We, as individuals, find a way to reach deep down inside and become exactly who we really are. This is beautiful!

Death has a way of bringing out the best, not always right away, though. In time. It's important to understand this. Some people require more time than others, and as fellow human beings we need to let time work its wonders for others.

Can you imagine someone wondering why Brett Farve will not have a good game, or wasn't as good as he should've been as soon as next week? Just when should he "get over it"? TIME will determine that and so will Brett and only Brett. Trust me, it won't be long and we'll start hearing complaints. Those who have mourned will understand.

Life, death, time all mean the same thing, don't they? Kind of like 2+2=4. Death ends the time one has here on this Earth. We don't know when that time will be, either. Those who live every day to the fullest will never die. This is beautiful!

When we die, we are done doing what we do and we are done being who we are, but are we really done or will we soon be forgotten?

I will not dwell on death, but I will use it as a measuring device in my life. The more you are, the more you do, the more you become, the more you will be remembered, the more you will live forever through someone else. This is beautiful!

Christmas reminds me of the ultimate life, the life that suffered death yet never died. We all know the Christmas story and that is our true heritage to follow.

These past months have been very rewarding to me. I have experienced answered prayers, love and support from family and friends, goals set and obtained, just so many positive things surrounding me that I'm truly a "new man." It's like all I used to be is just so much more alive than it ever was before.

This little note is full of deep gratitude and Christmas greetings for all you folks, and, of course, one final thought on this topic: Death we all understand, is part of life, but how much of your life will be part of your death?

Merry Christmas and a Healthy and Happy New Year!

Dave

David L. Reed

Heart Dysrhythmias Can Be Harmless or Serious

Irregular heart action that causes changes in the normal heartbeat is known as a dysrhythmia.

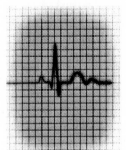

There are several types of dysrhythmias that can afflict various areas within the heart.

Bradycardias or slow heart rates - under 60 beats per minute - can occur without any symptoms and are frequently normal in very athletic people. When the heart rate becomes too slow it can cause dizziness, weakness, low blood pressure, sweaty, clammy skin and even fainting spells.

Tachycardias or fast heart rates - over 110 beats per minute - can cause symptoms of pounding, fluttering or racing feelings in the chest, neck, or throat and are known as palpitations. Some causes of tachycardias are brought on by lifestyle choices and include caffeine, smoking, alcohol, stress, sleep deprivation and exercise.

Ventricular irritability is a type of dysrhythmia that produces premature, extra beats between two normal heartbeats. An occasional premature ventricular beat is often harmless and can occur as a result of many of the same things that precipitate tachycardias. Frequent ventricular beats can be more serious and require treatment.

If you experience any of the above symptoms, please report them to your physician. Your physician is the best person to determine the cause of any dysrhythmia and recommend the appropriate method of treatment and

Journal No. 7 - February 1, 2004

So much has happened this past year I can finally say WOW!

This particular journal has been inspired for the innocent or the young ones who have yet to experience faults or vices. I'm thinking specifically of my nephews, nieces, grand daughters, godchildren, boys in scouting, LiT's in camp (Leaders in Training), and simply anyone who is still learning what life is all about. It is impossible to give this answer as I'm still learning myself and will continue to learn until the day I die. However, I can devote some tricks (facts) in life that may help you through your path walking days in front of you. Life is actually pretty fun.

1) Always tell the truth: You have no idea how much fun the truth can be. Truth has no consequences. You cannot get into any trouble when the truth is on your side. Other people will always admire you for not just telling the truth but living that way. It's COOL!

2) Save some money: Watching it grow is great! There's never enough. Money can be a very emotional and stressful subject. Ask anyone. So start saving some. Even a 12 year old can make $50.00 a month. Put away $20.00 of it every month and in 15 years I can show you a way to turn it into

$15,000.00 and a lot more. You won't even be 30 years old yet. This type of discipline will train you for all sorts of life issues and keep you in good shape when it's time to buy your first car or home or after high school education, even retirement.

3) Stay healthy: This particular subject has been proven time and time again and just recently by me. We may not be able to control our genes as far as what is in our body, but we can control the level of danger they may cause us by simply living a healthy lifestyle. As a young person, you may feel like nothing can stop you and, for the most part, you're right! Your bodies are becoming, if not already, the healthiest they will ever be. The trick is to keep them that way for the rest of your lives. There are some key things to remember. Yes, you must eat right. Yes, you must stay active and exercise. Yes you may think you're doing pretty good now; so did I when I was your age. Look what happened to me! I fell into a very common trap and never saw it coming because my stubborn youth wouldn't let me.

4) Don't drink, don't smoke, and don't do drugs: These are the worst things possible. I've never smoked pot or ever tried any drugs. If I had a second chance to change my past and was given a choice to take back anything, I wish I never had started smoking or drinking. Think about it. I'm sure you all have heard stories about this topic before and probably will many more times. In my case I'm getting that second chance and so far so good. You all think I'm doing pretty well with it, too, don't ya? Maybe so, **but it ain't easy**! Why start when you've seen the effect, the hold it has on someone. Did smoking and drinking give me heart disease? Not alone. It was in my genes. But heart disease can be created by smoking and drinking, and don't forget it. It is the number one killer of all the diseases. For those loved ones of mine in this Reed family circle, heart disease is in the genetic pool and looking for the next victim among

us. Don't fuel the fire by not keeping healthy. We may not be able to stop it, but we can fight and disable it and, more importantly defeat it. I hope to remain living proof.

Alcohol is also extremely dangerous in this family and many others. Look around you. Need I say more? This so-called social time or unwinding time is the biggest lie or UNTRUTH of all. You can't argue with anyone who has had more than their body can handle (how much is that?), let alone hold a real conversation for very long with anybody under the influence. Same with pot or any other drug, only difference is alcohol is legal. I'll bet the guys who wrote that law couldn't wait to go and have a couple! I wish I could honestly have a glass of wine or a beer again and leave it at that, **but I'm afraid to find out.** That high feeling is extremely controlling and I don't want to give in to it ever again! Do you really want to start? I remember my first beer; I was 14 and had a fun, hard day of work with my dad. Some of my best times were with him and naturally Dad said, go ahead, son, you earned it. I wonder had he known what my future held if he would've handed me a bottle of water instead. Or was he under the spell of alcohol and the high? We'll never know. He died at the early age of 51. What a waste, what a loss, and what a lesson!

I'm sure there are some people out there that can be in control of this but these same people will also from time to time lose control. This brings me to another point about "the high."

5) Self control: Since I've quit and since I'm past the cravings, my thinking has never been clearer. My mind actually works without a hitch or fogginess and my memory is back. That's why I can honestly say I'm not judging anyone who drinks. Actually, I'm jealous of those of you that can have one or two and walk away. I understand exactly what those of you "who indulge" are going through. I have no magic words for them. They already know that they don't have a problem, just ask them! Maybe they'll even tell you the truth, so don't ask them until midmorning. Truthfully, they know

45

what they have to do, but it's very difficult. No excuse, but difficult. If only they could feel the feeling of freedom, and self control. Of all the new experiences I've had this past year, this is the best of all. Quitting smoking has also been extremely rewarding. I can breathe again and I can smell again. Boy, do I ever smell again!

6) Be in charge of you: You really can be all you want to be. Just set your goal and make it reachable and just do it. There is nothing you can't do if you really want it bad enough. When you fall down, get back up. Always remember that good is stronger than evil, don't forget it. Follow that heart of yours. If a decision makes your heart feel good, then it is a good decision.

7) That's His day: **GOD**, if you don't know him, get to know him. Nothing will ever be without Him, except unhappiness and everything that goes with it. Ask Him for help, and then listen.

Well, that's kind of a quick list of do's and don'ts for a happy and healthy lifestyle. I hope you can understand and find your own way. Life is not meant to be scary, unfair or difficult. We, for the most part, are the so-called normal ones and find many ways to screw up our lives. What about the child born from drugs or alcohol or some other kind of deformity or disease? How would you like to fight those odds and/or live that lifestyle? These seven points can help all of us at different levels.

For the sake of conversation let's break down our aging process to five levels:

1) Very young, 0 - 20 years old, the learning years

2) Young and strong, 21 - 35 years old, the becoming years

3) Middle aged, 36-66 years old, the established years

4) Retirement years, all the past setting us up for this time in our lives

5) Old age, are we ready to say goodbye and then again hello to a new life

This is one way to look at the aging process, many books have been written about this subject and theory. This just happens to be the way I see it. I think all seven points, however, can be used during each one of these age levels. It gets harder to accomplish, though, every step of the way.

The one thing that helped me through it, other than an answered prayer called heart disease is this: my childhood. I went back to those days of learning and growing up, and could see a fresh beginning. I thought, wow! What's the difference between that person and me right now?

Other than some bad habits and 25 to 30 years later, deep down that same kid is still very much alive. All I had to do was want that bad enough and go take it back. I'm doing that and living that right now. I'm trying to tell all of you how good it feels to have my life back. I'm telling you young folks, don't go through the hell I went through. You can be anything you want to be right now if you make up your mind to be you and not someone else. I'm telling all you other people, if life has some kind of negative hold on you, take it back. You can, no matter what it is.

Walt Disney's four words to success: **Dream** your dreams and always **Believe** in those dreams. **Think** about your dreams often. **Dare**, yourself to follow those dreams.

A while back I wrote a journal about the word "lucky" and pretty much beat the crap out of that word and in closing used that word to describe myself later. I believe that I am the luckiest man alive! One of my brothers told me that I should be 'cause I've "earned it." Well, brother, haven't you?

I'd love to hear from you.

Take care and live well. I dare ya!

Dave

David L. Reed

Congestive Heart Failure Usually Controlled with Treatment

Each of our organs has a specific job to do to keep our bodies functioning properly.

One of our most important organs, the heart, pumps blood throughout the body, removing waste products and providing nutrients in the blood pumped through our blood vessels. Heart failure occurs when our heart muscle is not working efficiently. The heart muscle may be damaged or overworked. Congestive Heart Failure (CHF) means that this inefficiency is accompanied by a buildup of body fluid, usually in the legs, ankles, or lungs. The most frequent cause of congestive heart failure is coronary artery disease – narrowing of the arteries that supply blood to the heart muscle.

The best treatment for congestive heart failure is prevention. This means diagnosing and treating high blood pressure, eating right, regular exercise, weight control, not smoking, using alcohol in moderation if at all, and not using cocaine and other illicit drugs.

Treatment for congestive heart failure usually requires rest, proper diet, modifying daily activities and drugs. In more serious cases, heart surgery or heart transplants may be required. Most cases of mild and moderate congestive heart failure are treatable. With proper medical supervision, people with heart failure can continue to lead full lives.

Journal No. 8 March 5, 2004 – One Year Later and Over 1100-Miles Walked

This has been, without a doubt, the best year of my life. Being in good health and getting in shape is truly remarkable.

Recently, at my one-year check-up, Dr. Wallmeyer came in the room, looked at me, smiled and said, "David you look great"! Then he looked at his own midsection and said, "I need to lose some weight and start exercising again." That was probably the most rewarding comment I could ever receive from one of the men that saved my life! When he finished reading my chart and listening to my request on changing my medications to a smaller/lesser amount, he again smiled and agreed with that. He immediately wrote out two entirely new scripts, one to wean me off the beta-blocker, and Niaspan (a vitamin not a drug) vs. Zocor. Then we sat and chatted for a while. He was very pleased with my goings on and newly formed habits and told me to continue doing what I'm doing because it's working. "Of all my patients," he said, "I've finally got one that listened." We relived a couple of those moments from a year ago, and like all busy people enveloped around their own lives and work, the moment of glory was acknowledged and over between the two of us. Twenty minutes of the greatest satisfaction I believe I have ever felt. The tears I wiped from my face as I drove away from the area were, and still are, tears of joy and pride.

Some of you, and maybe most of you, will never know how I feel right now, and that's too bad. I mean, the way and how and what I went through to have this feeling, I wouldn't wish on anyone. However, the feeling of this kind of personal success is truly awesome, magnificent, rewarding, and cool. You get the idea. There are no words to describe how I feel right now. The look in my honey's eyes comes close. OOOH LA LA... Janey knows!

It helps to have more than one reason to change your lifestyle and I can honestly say it is true, and all those goals I set for myself in rehab and in my new life have been obtained. The hardest goal for me is, was, and **always will be** to live a controlling lifestyle over heart disease and to never have to go through this madness again. Dr. Wallmeyer looked me in the eye and said, "if you keep this up, living the way you are now, I don't see the need or reason to ever think you'll have a second bypass surgery." I know there is no guarantee, but that was music to my ears and the magic words to support this way of life forever. I will see him again on an annual basis "to talk," as he said, "and in about seven years will do another stress test to see how things measure up." I never cared for doctors before. This man, and his team are something extra special!

You know the feeling when deep down you just know that you're 100% all right? I've got that feeling right now and it was worth every step that I walked in the heat, snow, wind and rain; every calorie burned with thousands of calisthenics; every beer or drink turned down; every cigarette not lit; every can of pop not opened; no regular coffee in the morning, or any caffeine for that matter, and, of course, no more of the tons of sodium laced fat crap I used to eat. This is how you **beat heart disease**. And always remember, it doesn't go away. It's just laying deep down inside you waiting for each time you mess up your diet or smoke or drink **too much**

alcohol. It keeps track of every harmful thing you put inside your mouth and it takes advantage of your laziness and excess pounds if you don't exercise properly and often. It sounds pretty awful and scary, does it not? Kind of like a disease eating you up over time. That's exactly what it is and how it works in a non-medical way of explanation. I truly hope you never have to go through it. On the other hand, I would highly recommend it to some.

The bottom of the barrel looks different to all of us. Only your own heart, mind and gut know when and where the bottom lies. Don't pull others down with you. I know it's easier said than done, but I do believe the person hitting that so-called bottom already knows he or she is there and just needs to find that something to start the ball rolling. Funny thing is, everyone has someone that loves him or her and therefore someone to hurt. A good sign to each of us is, when those around us are hinting, questioning or downright being blunt about any one or more issues, call a time-out with yourself and reach down just as far as your ego will let you and do some soul searching. I hope you can see what others see. Then, and only then, can we understand what we (as individuals) have been seen as by those significant others and now the process of self-evaluation and correction can begin.

That's what this past year has been like for me, not just getting healthy physically, but mentally. After all, I grew up with this code of ethics: Physically strong, mentally awake and morally straight. That goes back to when I had life by the horns and the whole world was right there in front of me. Very shortly after that time, when I received the honor of Eagle Scout, my decisions in life and choices that I made were not the best I could have made.

I now understand and see the what, why and how. So, I had 26 years of hard knock schooling and maybe the next 25 to 60 years I will reap the rewards of long-term studies! I look forward to the many new classes I'm sure I'll be studying before long. Don't get me wrong, that time of life, yes had some very rough times for me, the kind that take a long time to bounce back from, but I also had a heck of a good time. I'm not talking about all the partying either. I've got a beautiful daughter, two sons, two wonderful granddaughters, and my wife, a woman who has always believed in me. What more can a guy ask for? Well, there is always something more.

I've written a lot about my feelings and emotions. Hopefully some of these thoughts will help you think things through, if needed. Some might say I've been judge-mental and out of line, and that's fine. Too bad they've missed the whole point of these so-called journals. I'm the last one to point a finger at anyone, except at myself. These journals **have been shared,** not with those that "need to read" or "have a problem," but they **<u>have been shared</u>** with those I love and care for and anyone else who might find these words interesting or helpful, and that's that.

I'm very excited to say one of my writings, the sixth journal, "The Beauty of Death," will be the forward in a newly published book titled "The Impossible" around the 4th of July. Janey and I are looking forward (pardon the pun) to reading and seeing this whole thing develop into who knows what. The author, an old friend, hunting buddy and colleague, Dr. Timothy Dosemagen, told me after reading the piece, "Wow, pretty powerful stuff, Dave. Would you mind if I used it"? Dah, I don't think so, Tim. He understood it was all about life, not death.

 "What happens when you die is between you and God and your own faith or lack thereof." My Aunt Loraine (she's always been more like my older sister) told me that some time ago in a conversation we had while preparing her father's funeral, and I'll never forget it.

You see, the ugly of life is death for those who don't believe, and the beauty of death is **your life.** Face it, and I mean face to face. You should have nothing to hide, and if you do, **change it.** Oh, and by the way, **yes, you can change if you want to.** Live life to the fullest. Enjoy as much as you can make happen. I am not talking about partying from time to time either. That is a waste of time and, your life. Life is not made for you; you've got to make it for yourself. **I refuse to waste and abuse any more of mine!**

My mother has a way of introducing me to people that really shows her pride in me, "and this is my oldest son, David," or "that's my David." I would always get the royal treatment. Proud! Ma has always been very tough and strong when it comes to her own feelings and beliefs and she raised us accordingly. She always taught us to be tough and not to let anyone tell us otherwise. Stick to your guns, she'd say, or something along that line. If we'd get knocked down or hurt in any way, shape or form, she would, of course, make sure there were no broken bones or would get the bleeding to stop and make sure we were okay and then say, "that'll teach ya" or "get back up" or "you'll get over it." Ma taught us to be tough and strong. She should be a football coach! This is where I think I fumbled the ability to say no to the vices. I really believe that if you think you're so tough and strong, you think you are invincible and you believe you can control the use of nicotine and alcohol and eat all the salty rich foods, when, in reality, that stuff starts to control you and before long it bites ya. After having a couple of beers or smokes, whatever, you crack open another one or light one up thinking, "I can handle it." I'm glad I've never smoked pot or did any other kinds of drugs: I don't know what that would've been like.

I was lucky the disease didn't bite me harder than it did. So in a way I'm glad to be as tough and as strong as I am. It got me through this year. The neat thing I think is, after all this I'm stronger and tougher than ever before! I have learned my lesson, Ma. I'll take a **chance** and say thanks.

My sister says, "Life is just a chance anyhow." She explains, "You can have a great upbringing and still make some really bad choices or come from an upbringing that's awful and beat all the odds." She continues with, "we never know what is in someone's head or heart and why sometimes we do right or wrong. Examples: Brothers or sisters from the same family are often extremely opposite. Another example: Childhood friends that grow up together and share the same experiences yet look at the many differences between them. We just never know what people are thinking and how they're going to react to situations. "Chance" is an opportunity to make "choices" and sometimes we make the wrong ones no matter where people come from." That's cool, Sis. I think I'll take a "Chance on Life"!

Steve, my little buddy and stepson, has been another strong influence on my life. He looked at me that day of surgery and said, "welcome to the club, Pa." He also has heart disease. "You'll be fine. If I can do it, I know you can - **You just have to make up your mind**." This from the seven year old, 17 years ago, who, while coming out of leg amputation surgery himself, said, "Where's Pa? I want to go ice fishing." Yup, that's my boy! He's right. I'm proud to be his Pa and friend.

I hope this has not been viewed as "preaching" on my part. These have simply been my thoughts, shared with you while trying to get things straight in my own head (soul searching, right, Aunt Reedy?) **It's not easy turning over a whole new leaf on life! But it's worth it!**

These thoughts are in no way an attempt to change anyone's way of thinking or way of living. I do hope it at least stirred up some conversation between loved ones or friends or between you and God. I know, for a fact, he listens. More answered prayers, our girls will not be going to Germany after all, and, in fact, they are back here in Lake Geneva, hopefully to stay close for a very long time.

Well. That's about all I have to say, for now, except bet ya the Packers go to the Super Bowl this year! And it would be nice to see or hear some country western at halftime.

See ya out walking; it's a great place to think... and talk!

Gone Fishin'

Dave

Saturated Fat is the Main Culprit in Cholesterol

One of the primary causes of heart disease is high cholesterol levels.

C holesterol has been found to cause the platelets in the blood to become stickier. This means the platelets are more likely to stick to the walls of the arteries, causing a blockage and coronary heart disease.

The main culprit is saturated fat which is found in meats and certain plant foods like coconut. A diet high in fat, especially from animal sources, means that more free fatty acids fill the blood, These building blocks of fat can reduce the efficiency of the heart. Cholesterol levels when you were a teenager were probably around 150-160 milliliters. Then, as the amount increased, heart disease increased. Studies have shown that getting your cholesterol levels back to their teenage levels will not only slow heart disease but may actually reverse it.

Journal No.9 – March 22, 2004 - March Madness: It Continues

Dedicated to Our Friend, Roger Olsen, and his Family

March, to some, is muddy winter...
March, to some, is basketball...
March, to some, is baseball...
March, to some, is tax related...
March, to some, means the coming of spring
March, to us, has been crazy...

March 1998 – Grandpa died
March 2000 – Janey's unexpected hysterectomy
March 2001 – Janey rolled our Jeep and totaled it (black ice), no injuries
March 2002 – Mike ended his life
March 2003 – My heart surgery
March 2004 – Mike's second year gone and now:

This morning a very close friend of ours, Roger, passed away in his sleep. Several months ago he was diagnosed with colon cancer, had it removed, started chemo and then they discovered more cancer in the bladder in the form of sheets, not a mass like a tumor, making it difficult to detect. Roger was already in the hospital at this point because of an infection and he had no strength or drive to do for himself and none of us, including Roger, could understand why. Now we know.

Roger, otherwise known as "Putz," from the movie Grumpy Old Men, or the "Old Fart" as another one of our friend's daughter, Sally, always called him, has always been somewhat on the gentle side of things. His sense of humor was something special. Putz couldn't tell a joke to save the world, but man did he laugh when something struck him funny. Tears, quite often, flowed from his eyes with belly rolling laughter. I'll miss that. He died a very young 69. He, by no means, at least in my eyes, appeared that old. Not that 69 is old, but it is older than 40. Ten months from 70 and his mindset was still 40 something. He was still working full time until this hit him. This past summer at Tim's (his youngest son), wedding he danced and carried on like he was 50. He seemed to be full of life.

After surgery, removal of the original tumor, and during his first chemo treatments, he changed. The drive and strength to carry on or to simply take care of himself and eating had diminished. This caused great concern for his family and friends. All of us were pushing him and he was trying, yet just couldn't. It seemed as if he had given up.

I had given his family a copy of my journals a while back when Roger was feeling low and disgusted with himself. The entire family enjoyed it, so they tell me. Roger talked about it a lot when I visited him in the hospital. He told me he wished he could find the strength to do what I did but just was not able to. One day he even got up and walked a few steps even though it wore him out. He was proud and wanted to do it again but did not have the strength. He asked me why? I cheered for him and told him baby steps were okay for now. He was still dehydrated and being fed from a tube. I assured him it would get better and he would feel stronger when the infection he was fighting was gone. He wanted to show his family and all of us he could beat this. He didn't want to be a burden.

The very next day the doctor gave him the long face. That night when I visited I asked Roger if he had any fight left in him. His response was "a little, but I don't think I'll be going fishing with you this spring." No one knew what Roger knew. He was not even sure if he'd make it through the night. I blew that thought off, thinking he was just scared (rightfully so). The doctors were meeting with Roger and his family the next day to further discuss the situation. I figured six months to a year, with all the arrogant medical knowledge I have.

Janey and I went on our vacation to the Dells that next day. We came back to town that Thursday the 18th to go say hello and wish our Mike a happy birthday at the cemetery and to pick up Angel and Reina. We then went to see Steve, our son who works at Wal-Mart, to check on him and ran into Chris and Tim, Roger's sons. They proceeded to inform us that the doctor said a day, maybe two, is all he had left. They didn't know if Roger would make it through the week. That was nine days ago. I guess you could say that God and the doctor didn't agree. That extra time did its magic. The family had their chance to say goodbye, along with a lot of friends. I know Arlene, his wife, was glad to have their daughter, Amy, moving back home. All necessary arrangements were made. Chris, Roger's oldest, was able to read his eulogy to his dad. Dad smiled. All unsettled family matters were resolved. Peace was in the air.

Rogers's response to my question (any fight left?) was certainly a quiet man's way of fighting. He knew his time was up and was ready to meet God. He fought with dignity and his family is very proud of him. He showed all of us how strong and courageous he really was. He kept his life in God's hands saying, "the doctors said one to two days; I'll go when God says." He never gave up. He also wanted to pass when no one was looking, hopefully when they were all sleeping. He did and at home. This Is Beautiful!

I (we) thank God for the time we had with Roger. He was a very pleasant, kind and quiet kind of guy. He died March 22, the same day as our Mike. Arlene apologized for having the same day. What a woman! We'll be more than happy to share this day, as it will bring us together even closer as friends.

We'll see ya soon, Putz.   Later, you Old Fart!

This wonderful month of March is really becoming a topic around this household! Janey and I just got back from our annual trip to the "Dells" and we had a great time there this year. The memory of our past March trips will always be with us. I personally get emotional when I look at that chair Janey was sitting in when the phone rang two years ago and Carol told her that Mike was dead, he had shot himself at a hotel in Mukwonago. She may still be breathing, but I watched my wife die the worst death a mother can die. This is why I refuse to see the movie, "The Passion."

Our lives have been filled with the wonderful presence of God and Jesus. So many times we've needed them and that Spirit is always with us. How else do you think we survive? It still is not easy. Often it sucks. It never goes away!

My heart is doing great, yet the pains of sad and tragic memories will always burn. I thank God for this also. I believe heartaches can teach us many things, like humility and perseverance. Then they can turn into respect and love.

This March madness thing will pass some year, but for now it sure does grab our attention. We don't look for things either, yet, wow, one thing after another. I look at the positive side and find flowers popping up, the sun getting warmer, seventeen family members with birthdays and/or anniversaries, our annual week of vacation time that we spend together (with our fingers crossed), walleye running, trap shooting and the near beginning of camping season. I love spring, the time of rebirth and new life. Easter is just around the corner making the season and our heritage come together. I love this time of year! It is so great to truly be alive...

Our friend's passing certainly made me stop and reflect. I'm so glad that I have been given this second chance! We all know of, or have at least heard of someone in their 30s or 40s dying from cancer or heart problems and so many other illnesses. We just never know when or how or if it will ever be our own turn. This is why I can't stress enough about healthy living. This whole thing has been on what I have done and how I've changed my life. Now I want to be a little more blunt to you.

Fact: Nobody can predict what happens tomorrow

Fact: Living healthy will not stop cancer or a lot of other illnesses

Fact: Living healthy will, however, help prevent heart disease and other illnesses

Fact: You will feel good and so much better with yourself - quality of life is just as important as quantity. In other words, live long and feel good.

Fact: "It's my body, I'll treat it the way I want." Wrong! You belong to God.

Enough: Just changing a little something will help you. When you have that specific "whatever" handled, try another. Baby steps are good, you're always moving ahead. We are not on this earth for very long. For you fellow Christians out there, your body, mind and soul belongs to whom? Take care of it! It's never too late. Put your trust in God and he will help you help yourself. For everyone else, trust what the medical world says, not the advertisements. Don't let society drive you. Trust those that know what they are talking about. I used to be so pigheaded and stubborn. Don't be like that. It's a trap!

Some say live and let live. That's a cop-out. That comes from folks who don't want to help themselves. They've given up. I hope they can find the strength and courage to admit they have a problem and face it head on. That's the hardest step. I truly hope they don't wait and see what happens.

Might not get the chance! Some people just need a little bit of a push to get them started. Others have no clue, they're uneducated. Some folks find out where the fish are biting and actually **share** the how, where, what, when and why.

I'm 44 years old. I think-- heck I know, I'm healthier now than when I was in my prime. This past year has done wonders for me. Call it my second prime. I can't imagine anyone not taking advantage of this situation. Wrong! I have talked about or shared most of these journals with a lot of folks and I can't get over the many different views. I can categorize these views in five areas:

1) Already healthy: These people totally understand everything I'm beginning to learn. They have been very helpful and understanding. Unfortunately, even being healthy is not a 100% guarantee of not having some sort of illness down the road.

2) The unhealthy and they know it: I was in this category. We folks try here and there to break the bad habits and just need that extra push or that "something" to get it going. The danger is every day that goes by is another day that the "trap" has a hold on you, and another day closer to a painful, unpleasant old age, if we live that long!

3) The unhealthy and they deny it: These people scare me. I believe we should tell them in any way we can. As Christians I believe we owe it to our brothers and sisters of this world. This is difficult at best. This is my way of telling everyone. I will also do my best at setting an example.

4) The Old Folks: I will not put an age number down. I honestly don't have a clue. I told you about Roger already. Another good friend of mine, Bill, who is 70, (I don't have many older friends left) just had bypass surgery. He's doing great! He even quit smoking. After my surgery, I told him I wanted another 40 years or more. He told me this: "I'm 70 now and I don't have 70 more, but I want all I can get. Damn smokin' will kill ya." He has a great attitude. I hope and pray all goes well with him.

5) The Older Folks who figure they've been around long enough: Products of category No. 2. I really have nothing to say other than, God, please help me understand!

It has been very interesting for me these past 12 months or so, hearing so many different reasons why or why not to live a healthy life. So many different excuses! There are so many who have gone through some kind of treatment and still they fall back in the trap. Been there, done that. Never again, I pray. Again, I thank God. For those who know very well they need to do something before it's too late, Nike says it best, **"Just Do It."**

I'll always remember the thoughts I had months before surgery. I knew deep down something was wrong. I knew my lifestyle needed a major change. I didn't know that I had heart disease. I'm not sure if I even knew what that was. I vividly remember how the pains hit me. I couldn't walk 50 yards before getting winded and would have to stop and catch my breath. During this time I would have a very heavy feeling in my chest. It felt like a 2x8 across my chest from armpit to armpit with a dozen cinder blocks stacked up pushing against me (heavy pressure). My neck felt tight and stiff, along with shooting pains in my elbow flying down and out of my left wrist or fingertips. My mouth would go dry and I'd finally have to stop and catch my breath, as my breathing was short and fast. It would double me over and sometimes bring me to my knees. This would go on for several minutes. This started several months prior. I was able to hide and conceal this for a while as the pains only hit a couple times a day, then more and more. Finally that last week it progressed from every hour to every half hour and sometimes more. I hid it from the guys at work but, Janey, thank God, saw this and didn't give me a choice. Once in the hospital, oxygen helped and, of course, it went away. The story "My Present" begins. Just think, this wasn't even a heart attack. I hope I never feel what that's like. One of the doctors said I probably wouldn't have felt it. Chances are it would have been a massive one and I would have died on the spot!

Not my time...it was "His"!

I am a YMCA Camp Maintenance Director. I am responsible for the cleanliness, safety and well-maintained facilities for 15,000 campers a year. Camp has 250 acres, consisting of many buildings and program areas. Preventative maintenance is what I do. I've started bringing work home with me to practice a little PM on myself.

My story is as real as I can possibly make it. No exaggerations or false info. I hope anyone who reads this will get some kind of idea what heart disease is and how important it is to listen to and do what the doctors and the rehab folks say. I took it a step further and decided to make a full life change. I decided to take advantage of this situation and make the best of it. So far so good and I can't imagine changing. I don't want to put anything unhealthy into my body. I want to get into and stay in shape. I certainly don't want to go through this again!

Remember, you really are what you eat and drink, especially if you don't exercise daily. My friend, John, says this: "if you don't want to look like a pig, stop eating pig." Personally, I love a good pork chop.

If you're not sure about heart disease, have a heart scan and see your doctor. Talk to people about different foods or workouts. Don't hide painful or weird feelings. Maybe you should consider a healthier lifestyle. Ask GOD what to do.

I can't cure anything, but I can tell you how I dealt with heart disease.

Amen!

Dave

David L. Reed

Drug-eluting Stents – Another Breakthrough in Heart Care

A stent is a stainless steel mesh cylinder that is inserted into a clogged artery during a balloon angioplasty where a small, inflatable balloon creates a wider channel to keep the artery open to allow blood to flow. The stent expands when the balloon is inflated. The balloon is then deflated and removed. The stent remains in place, keeping the artery open.

Each year, more than one million patients in the United States are treated with balloon angioplasty, and approximately 20% of patients who have had conventional coronary stents implanted develop scar tissue within the stent leading to the need for repeat treatment.

In 2003, the Federal Drug Administration approved the use of a drug-eluting stent, a state-of-the-art method for treating blocked arteries. All Saints Cardiovascular Institute uses

Drug-eluting stents reduce the incidence of re-block-age by more than

90%

drug-eluting stents, which are coated with an antibiotic. This stent helps keeps the artery propped open while simultaneously slowly releasing the drug into the vessel wall. The drug helps halt muscle cell proliferation, which is the primary cause of scar tissue that can lead to restenosis or re-blockage of arterial vessels. This drug also reduces inflammatory cell activity in the vessel wall, minimizing the potential for side effects, which could delay vessel healing. Studies show that drug-eluting stents reduce the incidence of re-blockage by more than 90 percent, compared with a bare metal stent.

Staying heart healthy is important. To learn if you are at risk for heart disease, talk to your doctor.

Journal No. 10 – Easter Sunday, April 11, 2004

Hello, and what a beautiful day! It's cloudy and cold. There are a few snowflakes flying about and the wind has a winter bite to it. There are trumpets playing in all the area churches, Easter lilies and white garments decorating many homes and buildings, Christians raising their voices in song and praise to the celebration of our Lord's Resurrection. It's great to be alive! Easter always makes me feel good, but this year it is with an extra good feeling.

Two things and two books have rekindled a fire inside me. I'll explain the two things later. The first book: "My Present," since the last journal, I've contacted 1st Books publishing and have decided to share these journals of mine with the world! I truly hope someone will find something within this book to help him or her. I'm not a very educated man when it comes to school, business and politics, but I have had a lot of visits from grief and many other unpleasant happenings in my life. It's a heck of a thing to have experience in! These so-called experiences range from dangerous car accidents to parents and grandparents dying, to parents with Alzheimer's disease, to the death of close friends, to all sorts of medical traumas, like Osteosarcoma (bone cancer) in our youngest child resulting in one of his precious little legs being cut off and chemo leaving him with heart problems, to "you don't have endometriosis, you need a hysterectomy like now," to heart disease and bypass surgery, not to mention suicide, our oldest son taking his own life and a pretty good chunk of life from those of us left behind. What could possibly be next, I ask? Whatever it is, I now understand that God needed me to bear it, maybe, so I could share it.

The second book: While my buddy Roger was in the hospital during his last few days he had many visitors who popped in and out. Pat, a mutual friend, was reading him a book, one chapter at a time. One night while I was there, she gave me the same book, a second copy she had been saving for her daughter. I just looked at this book titled "The Purpose Driven Life" by Rick Warren, and said thanks. (I really mean it, Pat!) Well, I'm not one to read much. In fact, if it's not about fishing, hunting, camping, tools, or the Green Bay Packers, I don't usually even pick up a book, especially one on religion. It sat on my end table for a couple of nights and then I picked it up, opened it, read the first couple of sentences and, BAM, I was hooked. All my questions now have insight. I continued with excitement. I thought, "finally, someone understands."

Mr. Warren, the author, is wonderful! In my eyes he is a marvelous tool of God. I'm not quite done with it yet, although maybe tonight or tomorrow as there are just a couple of chapters left. His book is a must read and, as it says on the cover, it truly is a No.1 bestseller. In my opinion, it is much more than that! He reaches us through real life examples, which we can compare our own life experiences with. What have these two books and two things done for me?

1) They have opened my eyes again.

2) My thought process is on the right track and that feels great.

3) My new life is the most positive thing I have ever felt.

4) My understanding and/or acceptance of grief and other sad experiences are real and each and every one of them brings me closer to God.

5) I see people differently now. I ask, Lord, why did you introduce this person to me? This specific thought really helps me to become a better person. Sometimes I am too quick to form a first opinion. That, I've learned, is very prejudice. Prejudice is also the worst form of judging others, in my opinion.

6) Like some people I know, I'm not a college graduate or scholar, just a high school graduate trying to make a living. BULL! I take great pride in my life. I have a beautiful family, which is as tight and close as we can be for now. We still, each of us, need our own space. My job as a camp caretaker is now a career as Camp Properties Manager. Titles mean nothing. Just come for a tour of Camp. That can be my title.

7) I understand my purpose in life! To spread my story and to hear others is just one reason. If you've really read this story, you already know I have many reasons or "purposes in life."

Personally, church has not existed for me in a while, and I miss it! My excuses have been rather selfish. 1) Money, money, money, is all I thought they wanted from me. 2) The "family feeling" that church is supposed to provide, wasn't there any more. 3) When Mike died, I needed the Pastor and the congregation to surround and comfort my family and I.

After Mike's funeral, Janey and I met with Pastor, just once a week for only a few weeks, when I learned it would take at least two years for life to settle back in or for the grieving process to "get over." I totally misunderstood! I (we) will never have that same life again! We will never be the same as we were before March 22, 2002. That tragic moment in time has altered our lives forever. I know better than anyone how Mike's mom, dad and brother feel and yet I'm here to tell ya, no, I don't! I can't possibly totally understand how each of them feel. They can't possibly totally understand how I feel either. Each of us has and will continue to grieve and grow as we ourselves can allow. Two years does not cure or take away the hurt. However, time does allow the rest of the community and family members to step back into our lives, to again surround us, with love and support. Each passing event like Mike's birthday, Christmas, Easter, Halloween, Mothers Day, and all those times has a crushing, empty feeling that eats up our hearts. Then the beauty steps in. Angel and Reina, Mike's daughters! They are something extra special. Kind of like the miracle we need to live on.

This morning at Easter service, we witnessed the sacrament of Baptism. Angel, the oldest, asked me what they were doing to the baby and I quietly tried to explain. More explanation will be needed in the near future. We will need the proper help and guidance to answer this question, as both girls are not yet baptized themselves. As a grandparent you realize the mistakes you've made with your own children. Wisdom and experience tell us to get the proper advice before we blunder on! Yes, we miss their daddy something awful. They, Angel and Reina, are Mike, in our hearts, yet they are also their own wonderful selves.

Life has been emptier than I thought. I blamed this on Mike and I now realize he is not the only emptiness I've felt. I basically left the church because I felt that the church abandoned me. I, I, I, me, me, me...OOPS! I fell again! So I started smoking and drinking more. Why not? I had the perfect EXCUSE!

This brings me back to the beginning, when I said there were two reasons and two books. Heart disease and suicide are two reasons for anyone to stop and think. For me, these two subjects have been an awakening. Living through these past four seasons has also worked its magic on me. The Easter season and spring are both a time of rebirth and new life, and that is exactly how I feel deep down inside.

We all have a "Purpose." I thank Mr. Warren for sharing his thoughts and knowledge with us. I'm glad I didn't read his book until I was almost done with my little piece. I probably wouldn't have written it. I guess you have to read his book in order to understand my thinking here.

Things happen for a reason. I wonder if Janey and I would have gotten as close to those two little princesses of ours, or if they would have witnessed that beautiful baby boy be baptized today if their daddy was still here? I wonder if I would have gotten this healthy and in shape if not for heart disease. I wonder why I got heart disease and why at the young age of 43 vs. the normal 60's and 70's? I wonder why I didn't have a heart attack and why did I not die? The past year of my life has been full of questions. Questions, like these make us think. All the miles of walking, and this time spent writing down my thoughts, have given me the time I've needed to accept and understand these questions in my life.

 My eyes have seen so much, yet I've been blind. Now I try to find the beauty in everything I see. I can finally see two sets of footprints in the sand again. It took some time, but now, being in the right frame of mind, my world is a much nicer place. All those so-called problems, at home, or at work, or never enough money, have stopped ganging up on me. I no longer need to hide from these every day troubles in life. Therefore, I no longer need crutches like tobacco, alcohol, caffeine, and unhealthy foods. Every thing balances out now, for the better.

That is my secret to living a strong healthy life.

Happy Easter,

Dave

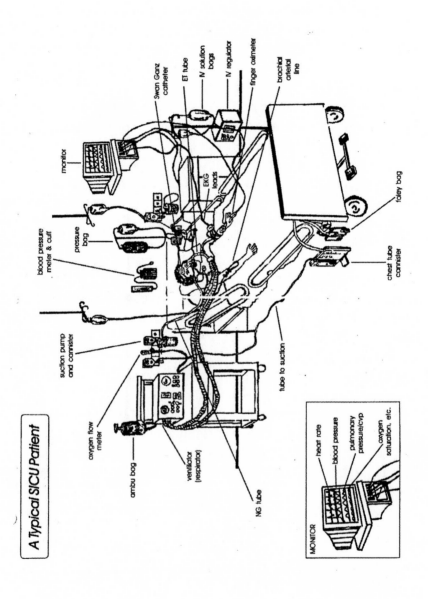

A Typical SICU Patient

How I did it:

One year ago I was diagnosed with coronary heart disease and had a quadruple bypass. I also dropped about 95 to 100 pounds and got in shape! I feel GREAT!

Everywhere I go people ask me, how did you do it? To sum it up in a couple of words, time and dedication, not to mention it was a true desire. Losing the weight and getting in shape is not, by any means, fun or easy. In fact, it's hard, but it certainly has its rewards. Setting a goal is one thing. Setting a goal and seeing it happen is totally awesome! Once it becomes a part of your life, it is fun, yet tough and challenging. The constant reminder of heart surgery is a benefit to me and hopefully my three scars, totaling 22 and one half inches, and my story can be a benefit to you.

*The first thing you need is at least two to three reasons why you want to change. One reason isn't enough; a second and or third can back up the first quite often and, believe me that happens a lot. My three reasons: 1) I didn't like what I saw in the mirror and I was tired of hearing comments from people about my gut. 2) I just didn't feel good, both physically and mentally about myself. 3) In order to control and live with heart disease, I need and want to do this.

*The people you live with sometimes make changing your lifestyle more difficult. They may not see things the way you do. Don't give up. What is your life worth? Do you understand the phrase "quality of life"? You will need to be greedy with your time. Explain to them your need and they will understand. They will cheer you on before long and may even join you. It may be difficult to start this, but once you do, you'll love it.

*Time is your greatest tool, or not. Heart disease does not happen overnight. It takes years to develop. Some day I'm going to write a book on all of this. This process of looking for a major lifetime result will take you the rest of your life to accomplish. Whether you have heart disease or if you're just trying to get into shape and live a healthy lifestyle, you must not treat this as a diet. Diets are for those who need to lose five to ten pounds. What I'm talking about is a total change in the way you think and live. Dedicate a daily time block. One to one and a half hours a day five to six days a week will make a major change in your life. You should shoot for five minutes of warm up, 45 minutes of cardio, 15-20 minutes strength training two to three times a week, five minutes of cool down stretches and, of course, a well deserved shower. I have two different routines for the week. Please don't think this is what you have to do. This is my schedule, and my time for me. Monday, Wednesday, and Friday, I hit the road for four miles walking, come back and do strength training and light calisthenics. Tuesday, Saturday, and Sunday I hit the road for five to eight miles and come back and do more calisthenics. Two days a week I try to get up extra early and do 20 minutes on the airdyne and 20 minutes on the treadmill, then go to work. Don't forget to do cool-down stretches after every workout. I usually take Thursday off. Plan ahead or you'll find yourself trapped into more than one day off a week. During vacations and times like that plan for at least a "maintain routine" (perhaps shorter and lighter) and that will get you by. Do not skip if at all possible. Time is everything. Use it wisely.

*Ease into your personal routine but stay with it and allow yourself flexibility as needed, either in time or in the activity(s) you choose. Everyone is different and have many different levels of self-discipline and self-control. It will take several times to actually get started with this kind of mind-set, and understand, it is all in your mind, and rightfully so because it's a major life event. The difference with this major life event and others is simple. It's your decision to do it, not something forced upon you to accept; in my case, an answered prayer and excellent rehab guidance. Your case, hopefully, will be self-ignited. Training is crucial. If you've never worked out before, try it with someone who does or buy a video, read a book, join a Y or health club and take an intro class. Why sweat bullets when you need to sweat calories!

The routine you choose is key. Remember, losing weight is not fun or easy, therefore, be sure you pick an exercise routine you'll enjoy. I love walking, biking and calisthenics and weights. I use dumbbells so I can work out one arm at a time or both at the same time, which allows me to adjust the toning process. Weight lifting, or strength training, as I was taught, builds up muscle. Most of us just need toning. Bulking up is your choice. There are many machines or presses available. Then again, a few simple dumbbell lifts will do the trick, but that's up to you and what you need. There's nothing wrong with a gym or some place to go. I simply prefer my own home. I lift my dumbbells two to three alternating days of the week. I lift four different weights. (25, 30, 35 and 40 pounds). After surgery, I had a 10-pound weight restriction, so I started with five pounds. Now I start with 25 pounds and do several different lifts 12 to 18 times each and rest 30 seconds in between each one. After that first set is done I rest for two minutes and then move on to the 30 pounds and do 12 to 16 reps each. The 35 pounds 12 times and the 40 pounds 8 to 10 times with the same rest times in between. I go up in weight every two to three weeks, by 5 pounds on the heavy side and adjust accordingly. I no longer increase weights due to the fact that my chest incision was starting to bother me. I came close to overdoing it. Takes me back to rehab training and knowing your limits. When I was a younger man, I could lift a lot more, but I guess I've aged, not to mention I've had my chest split open! Someone asked me, "what do you do with all the weights you don't use anymore"? Janey and Steve use them and eventually as I grow OLDER I'll need to go down in weight and sometimes a bad day comes along and I need to back off. You can always trade them in at a Play it Again sports shop.

Start your routine with five minutes of stretching. Then calisthenics. I do one to three sets of three much like weights, and reps. Push-ups, sit-ups and criss-cross style hand to toe touches, I start with 50 toe touches, then a 30 second break then 50 push-ups (45 degree angle style), then a 30 second break, then 50 sit-ups, rest two minutes, and then do it again. You can start out with lower reps and sets and adjust accordingly. There are many calisthenics and warm up exercises that one can do. Change them, from time to time. The idea is to just get loose before your actual workout begins. Even a steady slower walk will do the trick. Then I do 15 to 20 minutes on the airdyne (bike) at a 2.7 to 3.2 level and then 25 to 35 minutes on the treadmill walking at a 4.2 mph or 3.8mph with a 6.5 to 8 incline and occasionally I'll break out into a 6 to 8 mph run for one to two minutes and really get the heart pumping. Or I'm outside walking unless it is over 90, and/or ozone days, or below 15 degrees and not more than 20 mph winds and it 's not raining or snowing too hard. I walk three to four different routes to break up the repetition.

Some days I'll go for an actual bike ride, 10 to 12 miles. I do this when my legs or knees are sore from running and walking the day before and sometimes just to shake up the routine. When time allows, I'll do both, ride and walk, morning and evening. One last thing, I work out in the evening. However, I do the same stretches in the morning when I wake up. This really helps me start my day off good. It simply helps me get all my muscles and bones ready to face another active day. I'll bet, for you folks that work out in the morning, this would be worth doing in the evening.

*Nutrition: None of the above will go anywhere without the proper nutrition. We all need to decide what is comfortable for ourselves. Personally, I like the Omega 3 plan. You can purchase these books at Barnes and Noble for about $20.00. This book really educated me, on all the nutritional facts. You will be very surprised about some of the facts they give. My rehab dietitian says it's a very healthy plan and good for heart people like myself, better yet, a wonderful plan for anyone. It's not a diet as much as a **new way of eating**. One of these years, I hope, the FDA will be adopting this diet as the recommended diet for all. <u>You need to study and research all the different weight loss plans out there, and, remember, moderation and portion size is the key to any so-called diet.</u> Fiber is also a big part of my diet, and water. Very low sodium, low saturated fats, if any, and low cholesterol is key to heart healthy foods, and drink. Everyone I know who does not eat heart healthy can't believe there is anything left good to eat except Jello and salad. First off, you need to change your way of thinking where meals and "eating" are concerned. Second, there are more "good foods" available than you think. Talk to different people who eat healthy and get an idea or two from each and I guarantee you'll find things that appeal to your taste buds. Read a book or magazine on healthy eating. There are many to choose from.

Consider all these factors before deciding what to do. Don't forget to reward yourself from time to time. I like those No Name Sirloin Steaks. They are deceivingly small, yet tasty and the nutritional chart is not that bad. Their salmon steaks are even better. I really enjoy Natural Ovens Bakery products. I eat their products daily.

*Alcohol will screw-up any weight loss plan as it really messes with your triglycerides and metabolism. A glass of wine or two is okay or whatever it is you drink. One to two ounce servings of alcohol are actually approved by the medical world but no more. The catch with this particular subject is rather interesting. I'm not going to pick on the industry, but it's funny how every food and drink has some kind of common nutritional chart on its label or package, yet alcoholic beverages are very vague at best with their contents or serving size, i.e., beer. I don't remember offhand how to convert 4.5% or 5% by volume into one to two ounces. I do know that there are eight fluid ounces per serving, which in my head says 16 ounces is okay, which means two 12-ounce cans is more than the doctors say we should have, yet what about the shot of Jack? How is one to know?

Alcohol and I used to be rather close. I really enjoyed it. I used it to celebrate, to mourn, to socialize, to eat with, and simply just because, all too much, and all to often. People, this is a problem area for many of us. I used to think that I deserved a drink after a long day at work. I earned it. The key words here are "a drink." That means one or two. Alcohol can be used with good sense. Alcohol can also be abused and grossly misused. Many wonderful relationships have been destroyed because of alcohol. Please, be careful! Personally, I have to admit, I'm not sure if I can follow my own advise on proper consumption, so I just will not drink it anymore. I've already gone an entire year without...why start now?

*No matter what, **you must quit smoking.** This is most important. Next to genetics, smoking is number one on the hit parade when it comes to heart disease. There are many programs available to help us. Try them all if needed. This is required or you will be miserable for the rest of your shortened, unhealthy life! I tried several methods to help me stop and each time I tried one I felt I was getting closer to quitting. Finally, the do or die theory did it for me. Why wait for that?

*The benefits are really cool! The energy I have now is comparable to my high school days. My balance is back. I seem to have more tolerances for long lines. I love going to the grocery store. My senses are working again. I love smelling the outdoor seasons of Wisconsin. I really enjoy the comments and glances from all sorts of people. That was one of my reasons in the beginning if you recall, along with how I felt about myself.

I just had a full blood panel drawn a couple of weeks ago and my Doctors are very impressed. Every single item was perfect. My HDL (good cholesterol) could be a little higher, but my LDL (bad cholesterol) is nice and low. Overall my total count of 129 is very good. My weight is 205 this morning, a long way from where I was a year ago at 292, and November of 2002 I was over 300! My blood pressure is under control at 116/78. I no longer take any medication, just an aspirin a day and a couple of vitamins. A year ago I was in size 46 pants and 2XL shirts, now I wear size 36 pants and large to extra large shirts. Perfection (lack of another word) will come in time, continuing with proper diet and exercise. So the second and third reasons are being acknowledged also. My back seldom gives me problems, which has been a huge burden for a long time. The best part, when I look down, I see things I haven't seen in years, yup, my toes!

I FEEL GREAT!

Good Luck and Good Living.

Dave

The Last Page:

Most books have a final chapter putting an end to it. These stories end up with some sort of conclusion, whether it's a happy or sad ending. Some even leave us with unanswered questions or a desire for more. This little book does not have an ending. It is about to run out of pages and words to read, however, "My Present" will never end. Yours won't either, until you stop breathing.

Heart disease is very, very serious! It is a major killer for all ages and both sexes. Having a heart healthy diet, avoiding high blood pressure, no smoking of anything, daily exercise, weight loss, minimal alcohol intake, and not using drugs will help prevent the risk of heart disease. Take care of your heart and your heart will beat hard and strong for you. It will keep that clean, vital blood supply pumping throughout your entire body. This will also help keep many other harmful illnesses away.

I have totally changed my life, both physically and mentally. These changes, I believe, go hand in hand. Do not let this intimidate you. I'm as stubborn as they get, when it comes to breaking habits. I will be very honest with you. This past year, and everything included, has not been that difficult to overcome. It certainly has had it's up and downs, but, looking back, I could and would do it over and over again. Three keys: 1) Accept the facts and the truth. 2) A little prayer goes a long way. 3) Just do it. Some questions to ask yourself: Am I healthy? If not why not? What am I going to do about it or have I given up? Finally, when are you going to start?

I've been humbled again. Since the start of this little book of journals, several people that I know have made some wonderful comments to me, along with actually starting their own heart healthy program.

I intend to keep writing my own journals. However, this is as far as I wish to go publicly. I think it's hard to read long books about someone else's life. Maybe you are reading this while lying in a hospital bed, either before or after some kind of surgery. Maybe someone who cares for you gave you this to read. Maybe you are just bored with your life. Whatever the reason, remember this:

A year ago, I was very shy. I was embarrassed with myself. I was ashamed to talk to people. I felt diseased and disgraced. I was very overweight and had many bad habits. How could I have let myself go for so long? Heart disease, a quadruple by-pass and rehab helped me overcome those feelings and fears. Those involved reminded me that attitude and courage mean everything. They also told me exactly what I had to do to survive. One morning, I looked in the mirror straight into my own eyes, and for the first time, saw the partner God gave me to help. I wish I'd have done this earlier in my life. Regardless, I have done it and I feel fantastic! I am now very happy with my life and I am ready for the next challenge.

Yesterday is gone.
Tomorrow isn't here yet.
So, here's to "My Present..." and yours.

David L. Reed

About My Brother
By Mary Manka

This book is a story about a man that I have watched this past year turn his life around and make us all very proud. He has been nothing but brave, determined and genuine in his quest to help not only himself, but all of us as well. He could have just done this on his own and went on his own way, but instead he has taken us with him on his journey and continues to make us all a part of it. I'm not sure many people could take this route, but he did. I am grateful to him for sharing his life's journey with us. I know changing the life that he's had for 43 years has not been easy for him. He has been extremely determined and committed to take that second chance and use it to its full ability. Watching him do it with ease and gracefulness, knowing how hard it must have really been for him, has made me want to be a better woman! He has not complained or wavered in his journey.

I know Dave has always tried to live a life of putting other people first and helping others when in need. He has always been there for all of us. For a heart that was in trouble, you sure wouldn't know it. Dave wants us all to learn from it, including family, friends and even strangers. Not many people put their heart out there like that, but then again, we are talking about Dave.

My brother Dave is an example for all to see. Some people go back to their old ways and habits after something like this, but Dave did not. He saw the opportunity to take the second chance that was given to him and did not take it for granted. You see, our dad did not have a second chance that we know of, and I know we all wish he would have. Not everyone takes this precious life as serious as Dave has.

I am blessed to have spent quality time with him now a year later. My "big brother" is teaching me about the finer things in life, like a brother should. I believe my brother Dave has always tried to show me the right way to live, but now he is actual living proof of that and that makes it much easier to believe in someone. I am incredibly proud and happy to see him finally come into his own and living a lifestyle that everyone should.

I hope by reading his book you find yourself a little closer to the right path. God wants us all to cherish our bodies and our souls. My brother is doing that.

DAVID L. REED

David was born in Kenosha, Wisconsin and continues to reside in Southeast Wisconsin with his wife of 18 years, Janey. He has a daughter, Jennifer who is married to Brian; a stepson, Stephen who is engaged to Jennie; a stepson, Michael who is deceased; and two beautiful granddaughters, Angelica and Reina, who affectionately call him their Bumpa.

Reed grew up in a large Catholic family of 6 children. David always accepted the responsibility of oldest sibling and took it very serious, even as a young boy. This responsibility groomed him for his leadership roles later in Boy Scouts and in life in general. He served in many different positions while a Boy Scout, earning the highest honor as a youth, Eagle Scout, and again as an adult serving at troop and district level in many different roles, being recognized for his efforts, among others, the District Award of Merit and the Southeast Wisconsin Council's Silver Beaver award.

David attended St. Mary's High School in Burlington and Central High School in Salem, Wisconsin and attended Gateway Technical Institute in Kenosha, Wisconsin, working toward a degree in Horticulture and Landscaping.

After working in several different fields, including Boy Scout Camp, odd jobs, landscaping, carpentry, bait and tackle, food vending, and power line tree clearing, Reed was hired as Camp Caretaker at YMCA Camp MacLean in 1989, where he is still employed. Once again his leadership skills have proven to be a valuable asset for him. The position at Camp MacLean has grown and he is now Properties Manager/Maintenance Director. David is general manager of all new building projects and remodeling projects, as well as overseeing his staff in the custodial and overall maintenance of the camp.

David's new lifestyle includes spending time with his family as often as possible, his exercise routine, which includes walking, running and working out at least six days of every week and writing. He also likes to golf, hunt, fish, camp and anything to do with the Green Bay Packers.

Mr. Reed's first book, '*My Present*...' is due to be published in the fall of 2004.

Printed in the United States
23410LVS00006B/127-225

9 781418 495381